Mastering Dealership Appointments

Essential Car Sales Training for BDC and Internet Sales Teams

A Dealership Training Manual

Christopher Cunningham

Chapter I

Copyright

Mastering Dealership Appointments
Essential Car Sales Training for BDC and Internet Sales Teams

Copyright © 2024 by Chris Cunningham
All rights reserved.

No part of this publication may be reproduced, distributed, or transmitted in any form or by any means, including photocopying, recording, or other electronic or mechanical methods, without the prior written permission of the publisher, except in the case of brief quotations embodied in critical reviews and certain other noncommercial uses permitted by copyright law. For permission requests, please contact the publisher at the address below.

Publisher
IntelaTek, Inc.
Vass, NC, USA
www.IntelaTek.com

Disclaimer
This book is intended to provide helpful and informative material on the subject matter covered. It is sold with the understanding that the author and publisher are not engaged in rendering legal, financial, or other professional services. If legal advice or other expert assistance is required, the services of a competent professional should be sought.

Printed in the United States of America
First Edition: 2024

Table of Contents

Copyright 2
Preface 4
Introduction 5
   I. The Importance of Appointment Setting in Dealership Sales 6
   II. Understanding Customer Mindset and Buyer Behavior 16
   III. Energizing Your Call Performance for Maximum Impact 29
   IV. Appointment Setting Techniques 37
   V. Handling Objections and Delays 48
   VI. Confirming Appointments and Maximizing Show Rates 57
   VII. Follow-Up Strategies for No-Shows and Rescheduling 66
   VIII. Building Long-Term Skills and Success 79
   IX. Measuring Performance and Continuous Improvement 86
   X. Utilizing Technology in the Appointment Process 98
   XI. BDC (Business Development Center) Considerations 110

Chapter I

Preface

After over 25 years of experience in sales management, training, and leadership across various industries, I've seen firsthand the incredible power of a structured, consistent sales process. My journey has taken me from leading the largest satellite TV sales team in the U.S., as sales director, and leading the largest cost containment business consulting firm, in the country, as Sales and Marketing Director, to founding IntelaTek, a Nationwide sales training and business development firm, where I trained thousands of sales people, and sales managers, and my team set over 20,000 B2B sales appointments. Through each role, I've focused on building sales processes that produce measurable results, empower teams, and improve every facet of the sales experience.

My recent years in auto dealerships, serving as a sales manager, finance manager, and finance director, allowed me to see gaps in how dealerships manage leads and appointments. I recognized a lack of systems that provide real-time visibility into what's happening on the sales floor, from lead handling to final deal closure. It was this realization that led me to develop SalesLeader, the first Dealer Sales Management System, designed to ensure accountability and consistent execution of best practices from start to finish.

Mastering dealership appointments, specifically from inbound calls and online leads, is a critical part of a dealership's success, yet one that's often challenging to master. My goal in writing this manual is simple: to provide every sales and BDC representative and manager with the knowledge and tools they need to drive more qualified appointments into the showroom, reducing the advertising cost per sale, and maximizing the return on investment. This book is a guide to mastering the appointment-setting process, delivering consistent results, and ultimately driving greater profitability.

Welcome to *Mastering Dealership Appointments*. Let's make every lead count.

Introduction

When it comes to sales success in the automotive industry, getting customers physically into the dealership is everything. With every lead and appointment, there's an opportunity to connect with customers, understand their needs, and convert interest into a sale. But managing this process effectively requires a dedicated focus on appointment-setting skills, follow-up processes, and understanding customer behavior in today's digital age.

Today's car buyers are well-informed; they conduct extensive research online, compare prices across multiple dealerships, and often reach out only when they're seriously considering a purchase. However, securing a showroom visit often means navigating a series of common customer questions, handling objections, and creating a sense of urgency that makes them want to visit your dealership first.

As someone who's spent years refining sales processes across various industries and specifically in auto dealerships, I've learned that there are specific, teachable strategies that drive results. My experience spans managing sales teams that increased conversions by over 650% at the largest satellite tv provider, leading the country's largest cost-containment business consulting group, and, most recently, developing SalesLeader, the first Dealer Sales Management System that gives dealerships real-time visibility into their sales floor. These experiences have shaped the strategies I'm sharing with you in this book.

This training manual goes beyond basic phone skills and lead management. It is designed to give every dealership professional, from sales representatives to BDC agents and managers, clear, actionable steps to turn each call and internet lead into a confirmed, quality appointment. You'll learn how to answer customers' questions confidently, create urgency without pressure, and set appointments that result in showroom visits.

The strategies outlined here aim to help you master the appointment-setting process, improve show rates, and convert more leads into sales. With the help of this book and, where possible, SalesLeader, you'll be able to increase your appointment-to-show and showroom-to-sale ratios, maximizing the return on your dealership's advertising investment.

Chapter I
The Importance of Appointment Setting in Dealership Sales

Section 1. Importance of Setting Appointments That Result in Show-ups

In automotive sales, the difference between setting an appointment and having the customer actually show up is monumental. Each inbound inquiry represents a customer who has already invested time in researching, narrowing down options, and forming preferences. The decision to call or submit an online lead is often an indicator of heightened interest. However, without a well-executed appointment-setting strategy, even the most promising lead can slip through the cracks. Ensuring that customers follow through on their scheduled appointments is key to maximizing revenue, improving customer satisfaction, and driving dealership growth.

1.1 Why Show-up Rates Matter

Studies on customer behavior in automotive sales consistently show that the likelihood of purchase increases substantially when customers visit a dealership. According to industry data, approximately **41% of customers buy from the first dealership they physically visit**, and the average car buyer only visits **2-3 dealerships** before making a decision. This data highlights the urgency of moving potential buyers from a remote interaction to an in-person experience as quickly as possible. Each physical visit increases the likelihood of purchase by allowing the customer to engage with the car in person, which builds an emotional connection that digital platforms cannot replicate. When customers can touch, drive, and experience the vehicle, they often transition from "interested" to "ready to buy."

For dealerships, maintaining high show-up rates is directly tied to profitability. Each confirmed visit represents a potential sale and is an opportunity to convert interest into action. The appointment-to-show ratio is a key performance indicator (KPI) that significantly impacts dealership operations. High show-up rates reduce the time spent chasing down leads or scheduling follow-ups with no-show customers, allowing sales teams to focus on higher-quality interactions with motivated buyers.

1.2 The Cost of No-shows

The impact of no-show appointments goes beyond lost sales; it affects efficiency, morale, and overall dealership performance. No-shows mean wasted time and missed opportunities, as staff could have been working with active prospects. Additionally, each no-show requires re-engagement efforts—follow-up calls, emails, and rescheduling attempts—all of which consume resources that could have been invested in new or existing customers. By increasing show-up rates, dealerships can optimize resources and improve the effectiveness of their sales force.

1.3 Professionalism and Communication: The Foundations of Show-up Success

High show-up rates start with the quality of communication during the initial appointment-setting conversation. Appointment setting should not feel transactional; it should communicate value, urgency, and professionalism. Each interaction with a potential customer is a reflection of the dealership's brand and service standards. Professional communication instills trust, which is essential for gaining commitment. For instance, a customer is more likely to show up if they feel the appointment has been specially scheduled for their convenience, if their vehicle of interest will be prepped and ready, and if their questions will be addressed in person.

Communicating these benefits clearly, without overwhelming the customer, increases the likelihood of follow-through. Throughout this guide, we will introduce scripts and conversational techniques that convey respect for the customer's time and a sense of professionalism.

1.4 Strategies for Creating Urgency and Value

A customer's motivation to visit often hinges on the perceived urgency and value of the appointment. In a world where buyers can compare options at multiple dealerships within minutes, dealerships need to convey why their time is best spent visiting *your* showroom. Highlighting vehicle availability and demand, offering exclusive dealership services, and positioning the appointment as the optimal next step all help create urgency without unnecessary pressure.

Here are strategies to build urgency and value in the conversation:

- **Limited Availability**: Communicate the demand for the vehicle to imply that it may not be available for long. This could involve mentioning recent inquiries about the same vehicle or pointing out the high turnover rate on similar models.

- **Exclusive Benefits**: Highlight unique dealership services that the customer can only experience in person. Examples include personalized test drives, complimentary trade-in appraisals, and onsite financing consultations.

- **Personalized Attention**: Let the customer know their visit will be tailored to their interests. Mentioning that the vehicle will be prepped specifically for them or that a dedicated team member will assist them adds a personalized touch that increases commitment.

1.5 Appointment-to-Show Best Practices in the Industry

Chapter I

Dealerships with the highest appointment-to-show rates often follow a structured approach:

- **Immediate Follow-up**: Respond to leads within minutes of receiving the inquiry. Studies show that the probability of successfully connecting with a lead drops sharply after the first 5 minutes.

- **Clear and Simple Scheduling**: Offer specific appointment times instead of vague options. This shows respect for the customer's time and implies that the dealership is in high demand. Example: "We can schedule your test drive for either 2:00 p.m. today or 11:00 a.m. tomorrow. Which works better for you?"

- **Use of Multiple Touchpoints**: Confirm appointments with follow-up emails and texts that recap details, such as appointment time, dealership location, and contact information. Providing these details reduces no-shows by ensuring customers are well-informed and committed.

- **Reminder and Confirmation Protocols**: Sending reminders the day before and calling to confirm the appointment day-of establishes a high level of service and keeps the dealership top of mind.

Conclusion

Appointment setting is a blend of sales skill, psychology, and timing. High show-up rates aren't merely a matter of luck—they're the result of intentional and consistent practices. By understanding the customer's motivations, communicating with clarity and professionalism, and creating urgency, dealership teams can turn inbound leads into showroom visits, maximizing each opportunity for success.

In the sections that follow, we will outline practical techniques, scripts, and protocols that are designed to ensure every scheduled appointment leads to meaningful face-to-face interactions and increases the likelihood of a successful sale.

Section 2. Overview of the Unique Dynamics of Inbound Calls and Internet Leads

Inbound calls and internet leads are prime opportunities for dealerships to connect with customers who are already expressing interest in a vehicle. Unlike outbound sales, where dealerships initiate contact, inbound leads are a clear indicator of customer intent, often signaling a high level of engagement. Properly handling these inquiries can result in a higher show-up rate, as these customers are usually further along in their decision-making process. However, understanding and mastering the unique dynamics of these interactions is key to transforming these inquiries into appointments and eventual sales.

2.1. The Customer's Journey to Inbound Engagement

When a customer reaches out via phone or submits an online lead form, they've usually invested time in research, shortlisting vehicles, and often comparing options across different dealerships. They may have already checked out reviews, inspected dealership ratings, and formed initial opinions. This well-informed customer has expectations; they are not simply browsing but seeking specific information, reassurance, and a reason to visit your dealership.

However, even if a customer has done their homework, they may still be uncertain or hesitant about next steps. The decision to contact a dealership is often a moment of vulnerability, as they look to the dealership for guidance, expertise, and validation of their choice. Addressing this need promptly and effectively is essential to move them closer to scheduling an in-person visit.

2.2 The Impact of Timing on Conversion

The speed of response plays a critical role in converting inbound inquiries. Industry data reveals that the likelihood of reaching and converting a lead plummets as response time increases. Responding within the first five minutes is 21 times more effective than waiting even 30 minutes. Fast response signals a high level of professionalism and reinforces the dealership's commitment to customer service.

A widely cited 2007 study conducted by InsideSales.com in partnership with MIT analyzed 15,000 leads across various industries and found that responding to an Internet lead within five minutes increased the likelihood of qualifying that lead by a factor of 21 compared to waiting even 30 minutes. Since then, this "5-minute rule" has been validated by multiple follow-up studies, reinforcing that immediate responses dramatically improve conversion rates and engagement levels.

2.3. Best Practices for Timely Responses:

- **Immediate Response**: Ensure that a dedicated team or automated system acknowledges internet leads within moments of submission.

- **Prioritizing Call Answering**: Calls should ideally be answered by a live representative whenever possible. Avoid prolonged hold times or complex menu options, as these can frustrate potential customers.

- **Follow-Up for Missed Calls**: If a call is missed, follow up with a prompt callback, ideally within five minutes, to retain the customer's interest.

2.4. Differences Between Phone and Internet Inquiries

While inbound calls and internet leads both represent customer interest, they engage differently and require distinct strategies:

Inbound Calls: Customers calling the dealership are often seeking immediate answers. They may have specific questions about vehicle availability, financing, or features. Calls provide an opportunity for real-time connection, enabling sales teams to establish rapport, build excitement, and set appointments directly. Calls also allow for a more personalized approach, as representatives can gauge the customer's tone, interest level, and reaction to responses.

Key Strategies for Inbound Calls:

- **Listen First, Speak Second**: Begin by listening carefully to the customer's questions or concerns. This shows respect for their needs and sets a collaborative tone.

- **Use Active Language**: Statements like, "I can check that for you right away," or "Let's secure a time for you to come in and see it firsthand" convey assurance and keep the conversation moving.

- **Guide Toward a Decision**: After addressing their inquiries, guide them toward scheduling an appointment by offering two specific time slots within the next 24–48 hours. This approach keeps the decision simple and creates a sense of urgency.

Internet Leads: Customers submitting internet leads are generally comfortable with digital communication and may not expect an immediate response. They may submit inquiries outside of business hours or while browsing inventory, so an efficient follow-up strategy is crucial. The initial response should confirm receipt, acknowledge specific interests, and establish a clear next step—such as scheduling a call or visit.

Key Strategies for Internet Leads:

- **Automated and Personalized Response**: Send an automated email or text acknowledgment immediately, followed by a more personalized response within 15–30 minutes. Include the customer's name and reference any specific details they mentioned in their inquiry.

- **Multi-Channel Follow-Up**: Internet leads benefit from follow-ups through multiple channels (e.g., email, SMS, and phone calls). This ensures the customer receives the message in their preferred format and reinforces the dealership's attentiveness.

- **Direct Path to Appointment Setting**: Once a rapport has been established, suggest times for a call or appointment at the dealership. Offer flexibility and emphasize the benefits of an in-person visit, such as a personalized walk-through of the vehicle or the opportunity for a trade-in appraisal.

2.5. Establishing Credibility and Building Trust

Both inbound calls and internet leads are opportunities to establish trust with customers who may be wary of traditional sales tactics. Many customers have experienced high-pressure interactions at other dealerships or are cautious after researching industry practices online. Responding to their inquiries with transparency, warmth, and respect goes a long way in creating trust.

Building Trust Strategies:

- **Answer Directly and Honestly**: If a customer asks about a vehicle's availability, provide a direct answer and explain any potential constraints, such as limited stock or high demand. Honesty here avoids any potential disappointment and reinforces credibility.

- **Show Transparency on Price and Availability**: If discussing price, present a range or a ballpark figure if exact details are unavailable, and gently guide the customer toward an in-person appointment where they can learn more.

- **Create Familiarity with Personal Touches**: Use the customer's name frequently, reference their stated preferences, and personalize the conversation wherever possible. In follow-up emails, including the representative's photo, direct contact number, and dealership logo can help build a connection and make the interaction feel more genuine.

2.6. Creating Urgency Without Pressure

An essential component of handling inbound inquiries is creating urgency in a way that feels organic and non-invasive. Customers are often more motivated to take action when they perceive a benefit to acting sooner. However, over-pressuring a potential buyer can lead to pushback or even abandonment of the inquiry.

Strategies for Balanced Urgency:

- **Highlight Availability and Demand**: For vehicles in high demand, let the customer know that availability is limited without resorting to high-pressure language. Phrasing like, "This model has been popular this week," or "I'd love to reserve it for you," keeps the tone positive.

- **Promote the Benefits of Visiting**: Emphasize the advantages of an in-person visit, such as the opportunity to test drive, receive a trade-in evaluation, or access special financing options. Frame the appointment as a step that benefits the customer rather than the dealership.
- **Offer Appointment Incentives**: Some dealerships provide small incentives for showing up, like a free gas card, gift certificate, or car care voucher. Mentioning a small perk can encourage attendance and enhance the customer's perception of the dealership's hospitality.

2.7. The Role of Follow-Up in Securing the Appointment

The follow-up process is essential to confirm the customer's commitment and ensure the appointment is seen as a priority. Whether for an inbound call or an internet lead,

Chapter I

follow-up strategies help solidify the appointment in the customer's schedule, reducing the likelihood of a no-show.

Effective Follow-Up Protocols:

- **Personalized Reminders**: Send a friendly follow-up email or SMS within 24 hours of setting the appointment. Include key details such as the vehicle of interest, appointment time, and dealership address.

- **Day-Before and Same-Day Reminders**: Contact the customer a day before and again on the day of the appointment. This can be a quick text confirming the appointment and adding, "We're looking forward to meeting you!" or, "Your vehicle will be ready for you at your scheduled time."

- **Maintaining Flexibility**: If the customer cannot confirm or requests a reschedule, handle the request promptly and without frustration. Maintaining a flexible, understanding attitude increases the likelihood they will follow through on the new time.

Conclusion

Inbound calls and internet leads are golden opportunities to engage customers who have already shown interest in the dealership. Proper handling of these leads—through prompt responses, tailored communication, and strategic follow-up—can significantly increase the likelihood of converting these inquiries into confirmed appointments. By recognizing the unique dynamics of inbound interactions, dealerships can create positive, impactful experiences that pave the way for strong show-up rates and successful sales outcomes.

Section 3. Defining the Objective: Getting Customers Physically into the Dealership to Increase Closing Rates

The core goal of inbound appointment setting is to convert inquiries into dealership visits, as this dramatically improves the chances of a sale. The in-person experience offers a level of engagement, sensory connection, and emotional involvement that cannot be achieved through remote communication. When a customer steps into the dealership, they're not just another lead—they are a tangible opportunity. Effective appointment setting builds on this goal, making it as easy as possible for customers to move from interest to action.

3.1. Why In-Person Visits Are Key to Closing Sales

Industry data underscores the powerful impact of dealership visits on sales conversion rates. When a customer visits in person, the likelihood of purchase can increase by over 60% compared to remote engagements. This is because the physical presence allows the customer to immerse themselves in the experience, feel the vehicle's comfort, and imagine themselves owning it. The tactile and sensory experience, combined with professional guidance from a sales team member, helps bridge the gap between interest and decision.

In addition, customers who visit the dealership can experience the brand atmosphere firsthand, see the professionalism of the team, and interact with experts who can address questions and concerns in real-time. For many, this direct contact builds trust and confidence, both of which are essential for making a commitment to buy.

Example: Imagine a customer who has done extensive online research on a specific model, comparing specs and features. However, they're still debating whether the vehicle's interior is comfortable enough or if it drives as smoothly as reviews suggest. When they visit the dealership, they can sit in the driver's seat, feel the upholstery, test the handling, and immediately confirm that it meets their expectations. This physical validation of their research can be the deciding factor that leads to a sale.

3.2. Transforming Interest into Action

Moving a customer from a casual inquiry to a committed visit involves more than simply scheduling an appointment. It requires conveying a sense of excitement, exclusivity, and value that encourages the customer to prioritize the visit. The objective is to build on their existing interest and provide compelling reasons to move forward in their car-buying journey.

3.3. Strategies to Encourage Dealership Visits:

- **Highlight the Tangible Benefits of Visiting**: Instead of just inviting them for a test drive, mention specific advantages of the in-person experience. For instance, emphasize that test drives offer a unique opportunity to see how the vehicle performs under various conditions or highlight the expertise of the on-site team who can answer detailed questions about features and financing options.

- **Create a Personalized Experience**: Letting customers know that a vehicle is being prepared specifically for them enhances the feeling of importance and investment. Statements like, "We'll have the [Vehicle Model] ready for you to explore, and our team will ensure you get the best experience," give the impression that the dealership is going out of its way to accommodate their needs.

- **Stress Exclusive Benefits**: Point out any value-added services available only at the dealership, such as an exclusive trade-in valuation or limited-time incentives for in-person buyers. Offering something unique, like a quick appraisal of their current vehicle or personalized financing assistance, adds practical value and reduces the barrier to visiting.

3.4. The Power of Urgency and Scarcity in Driving Visits

Chapter I

Creating a sense of urgency is one of the most effective tools for motivating customers to visit the dealership promptly. People respond to the fear of missing out (FOMO), and when they perceive that waiting could lead to a missed opportunity, they're more likely to take action sooner.

Balancing Urgency and Pressure: It's crucial to frame urgency in a way that doesn't feel forced. The language should remain positive and supportive rather than overbearing. Instead of saying, "This car might be gone tomorrow," you might say, "This model has been very popular this week, so I'd recommend coming in while it's still available."

Example of Effective Urgency Statements:
- **Limited Availability of Popular Models**: "We've had a lot of interest in the [Vehicle Model], and I'd hate for you to miss the chance to see it while it's still available."

3.5. Building Confidence and Reducing Anxiety with Pre-Appointment Communication

From the moment an appointment is set to the time the customer arrives, consistent, friendly communication is key to reinforcing their decision to visit. Effective pre-appointment communication not only provides logistical information but also reinforces the dealership's professionalism, ensuring the customer feels valued, welcomed, and confident in their choice.

3.6. Pre-Appointment Communication Strategies:

- **Confirmation Emails or Texts**: Immediately after the appointment is set, send a confirmation message that reiterates the appointment details, addresses, and contact information, and includes a welcoming message. An example message could be: "We're excited to welcome you to [Dealership Name]! Your appointment to test drive the [Vehicle Make & Model] is confirmed for [Time]. If you have any questions, feel free to reach out to us at [Phone Number]."

- **Personalized Touches in Reminders**: Sending reminders a day before the appointment and on the day of helps reduce no-shows. Personalized reminders like, "We've prepped the [Vehicle Make & Model] for your visit tomorrow!" or "Looking forward to meeting you today at [Dealership]!" convey attention to detail and build anticipation.

- **Addressing Practical Details**: Include tips like dealership hours, parking information, and necessary documents (such as driver's licenses for test drives). This reduces any uncertainty the customer may have, making the visit as seamless as possible.

Conclusion: Maximizing the In-Person Opportunity

Chapter I

Getting a customer physically into the dealership is a strategic accomplishment that significantly increases the likelihood of closing a sale. The objective of every appointment-setting interaction should be to create a smooth, engaging pathway for the customer to experience the dealership and vehicle firsthand. Each conversation, confirmation, and follow-up message should build upon the initial interest, emphasizing the tangible benefits of visiting and setting the stage for a successful sale.

By setting clear objectives, building excitement, and maintaining consistent communication, dealerships can not only increase appointment show-up rates but also lay the groundwork for lasting customer relationships. This approach not only enhances the likelihood of closing a sale but also fosters a positive impression that could lead to repeat business and referrals, strengthening the des reputation and performance over the long term.

Chapter II

Understanding Customer Mindset and Buyer Behavior

Section 1. The Different Types of Buyers

Understanding the distinct buyer types in a dealership setting is essential for tailoring your approach and maximizing appointment show-ups and sales conversions. Buyers have varied motivations, and knowing their key influences enables you to adapt your sales strategy to meet each customer's unique needs. Here, we'll explore three common buyer types—Experience Buyers, Relationship Buyers, and Price Buyers—and provide actionable insights into what drives them to choose one dealership over another.

1.1 The Experience Buyer

Experience Buyers value the overall purchasing journey as much as the vehicle itself. For them, the process of buying a car is as memorable as the car they're purchasing, and they're willing to invest in a dealership that offers a smooth, enjoyable, and high-quality experience.

Key Influencers:
- **Customer Service**: Experience Buyers look for personalized, friendly, and attentive service. The staff's ability to engage and make them feel valued is crucial to creating a positive experience.
- **Dealership Atmosphere**: A comfortable, welcoming, and well-organized showroom can significantly impact their decision. Details like cleanliness, decor, and amenities matter to this buyer type.
- **Brand Reputation**: They often select dealerships with strong reputations, positive reviews, and a trusted presence in the community.

Sales Approach: With Experience Buyers, focus on providing an exceptional experience from the moment they enter the dealership. Make the process smooth and enjoyable, pay close attention to their needs, and show them that every detail has been considered. For these customers, hassle-free, memorable interactions are key.

1.2. The Relationship Buyer

Relationship Buyers prioritize trust, connection, and long-term association with the dealership and salesperson. They see their purchase as the start of an ongoing relationship rather than a one-time transaction.

Key Influencers:
- **Trust and Honesty**: Relationship Buyers seek a salesperson who is transparent, honest, and forthcoming with information. They want to feel assured that they're receiving reliable information.
- **Ongoing Relationship**: They place high value on after-sales service, follow-ups, and the dealership's dedication to long-term support, like regular maintenance reminders or check-ins.
- **Personal Connection**: These buyers want a genuine connection with their salesperson and dealership. Feeling valued and understood, rather than just another sale, is essential for them.

Sales Approach: Build rapport and take the time to understand their specific needs. Be consistent and honest in all communications, and ensure follow-up after the sale to establish a lasting relationship. Show empathy and a personal touch to reassure them that you're committed to their satisfaction beyond the sale itself.

1.3. The Price Buyer

Price Buyers are primarily motivated by finding the best financial deal. They seek competitive pricing and efficient, transparent transactions that allow them to feel they're getting great value for their investment.

Key Influencers:
- **Competitive Pricing**: They are drawn to dealerships that offer the best prices, discounts, or financing options.
- **Clear Value Proposition**: Price Buyers appreciate straightforward and transparent information about what they're getting for their money.
- **Efficiency**: Price Buyers typically want a quick, no-nonsense buying process. They prefer a straightforward experience without extensive upselling.

Sales Approach: For Price Buyers, it's best to be upfront about pricing, current deals, and financing options. Provide clear comparisons of value and costs to reinforce that they're making a smart purchase. Respect their preference for a straightforward transaction while ensuring you still offer attentive service.

1.4. Integrating Approaches

Although buyers may predominantly align with one category, they often exhibit traits from multiple types. For example, an Experience Buyer might still appreciate a good deal, or a Price Buyer may want a smooth, efficient experience. Adapting your

Chapter II

approach to accommodate these overlapping priorities helps ensure that every customer feels understood and valued. This flexibility not only leads to immediate sales but also strengthens the dealership's reputation, attracting a wider range of customers.

Section 2. The typical buying cycle for car shoppers (from research to purchase).

The car-buying process has transformed drastically over the past few decades. Today's customers can browse inventories, compare models, read reviews, and explore financing options—all from the comfort of their homes. Yet, not long ago, buying a car meant something very different: it was a hands-on, day-long excursion that often involved driving from one dealership to the next, examining the cars in person.

In the past, customers relied on newspapers and magazines to find local listings, and publications like AutoTrader were must-haves for anyone in the market for a new or used vehicle. I remember one specific instance back in 1989 when I was in the market for a used Corvette. My friend and I spent an entire day driving from dealership to dealership, hoping to find the right car. During one of these stops, we pulled into a used car lot and spotted a vehicle that neither of us could quite identify. Initially, I thought it was a Lamborghini, while my friend guessed it was a Ferrari. A sales rep approached, inserted the key into the side of the car, and the whole top of the car lifted up hydraulically. I was sold right then and there. It turned out to be a kit car, and while it was a thrill to own, I spent a lot of time fixing it. When it came time to sell, I listed it in AutoTrader magazine, and to my surprise, they asked to feature it on the cover. I still have a few copies of that issue, with my car prominently displayed across the front page, a keepsake of the days when buying and selling cars was a very different experience.

Today, finding a car is much simpler. Instead of dealership hopping, customers go on sites like AutoTrader.com, CarGurus.com, or Cars.com. With just a few clicks, they can enter the make, model, year, mileage, price range, and distance from their location, narrowing down to the exact car they want within seconds. It's fast, convenient, and provides a level of precision that was unimaginable years ago.

However, I find that customers today often spend more time researching vehicles online than they would have spent driving from dealership to dealership back in the day. While the research process was once limited to face-to-face interactions with salespeople and printed information, today's buyers have access to vast online resources, from consumer reviews to detailed videos. This has shifted the role of the salesperson; back then, it was about persuading the customer to buy what was on your lot. Now, it's about providing the expertise, guidance, and trustworthiness to help them confirm and finalize a decision they've often already started making.

2.1 Awareness and Initial Research

In this awareness phase, potential buyers are at the very beginning of their journey, recognizing a need or desire for a new or used vehicle. They might be influenced by lifestyle changes, a need for a more reliable car, or simply a desire to upgrade. Customers today start with online research—browsing websites, reading reviews, and exploring different models and features. They're forming general impressions and preferences, often with guidance from social media, car review sites, and word-of-mouth from friends and family.

Dealership Opportunity:

- **Educational Content**: Dealerships can tap into this phase by offering resources that address common questions and introduce them to the dealership. Articles on topics like "What to Look for When Buying a Used Car" or "Top Safety Features in 2024 Models" help establish the dealership as an authoritative source.

- **SEO and Online Presence**: A strong online presence, including well-optimized search engine results for local keywords, ensures the dealership can be easily found during the early stages of a customer's search.

2.2 Consideration and Narrowing Options

Once customers have explored options, they begin narrowing down their choices. They've likely settled on a vehicle type (such as SUV or sedan) and are looking closely at specific models and brands that meet their needs and budget. They'll start comparing features, specs, prices, and more to find the vehicle that fits best.

This phase marks a shift from general curiosity to focused consideration. Back in the day, this might have meant driving from one dealership to another, hoping to find that dream car among the options on each lot. Today, customers can easily access side-by-side comparisons online, allowing them to make more informed decisions without needing to visit multiple locations.

Dealership Opportunity:

- **Responsive Online Engagement**: Today's customers may reach out to dealerships during this phase, submitting online inquiries to ask about availability, pricing, or test drive options. Quick, helpful responses that address their specific questions make a strong first impression.

- **Virtual Showroom and Detailed Listings**: Well-organized online listings with high-quality images, videos, and detailed descriptions enable customers to explore options remotely. It's a way to offer the same guidance and excitement of a showroom visit, from the convenience of their home.

2.3. Decision and Pre-Purchase

Chapter II

The decision phase is when the customer has honed in on a specific model and is ready to make a choice. Back in the day, the "decision" was often made on the dealership floor, sometimes with the sales rep nudging things along. Today, however, the decision is frequently made before a customer steps into the showroom. The goal is now to confirm the decision with a test drive, negotiate terms, and secure financing. This is where the dealership's role shifts to providing assurance, transparency, and flexibility. Customers may enter this stage with certain expectations around pricing or trade-in value, so managing these expectations with transparency is crucial.

Dealership Opportunity:

- **Creating a Positive Test Drive Experience**: Ensuring the car is ready, clean, and equipped with a full tank for a smooth test drive experience can leave a lasting impression. A well-executed test drive can be the final nudge a customer needs to feel certain about their choice.

- **Transparency in Pricing and Terms**: Today's buyers expect clear, upfront information. Avoiding surprises and providing transparent pricing helps reinforce trust and prevent any last-minute doubts.

- **Flexibility in Negotiation**: While the internet provides price transparency, dealerships can still offer value by accommodating financing options or discussing warranties and other incentives that make the deal more attractive.

2.4. Purchase and Delivery

At this final stage, the customer is ready to make the purchase. In the old days, this might have involved several rounds of negotiation on the showroom floor. Today, customers are generally well-prepared and aware of market values, often leaving little room for haggling.

Dealership Opportunity:

- **Personalized Handoff**: A thorough vehicle walkthrough, feature demonstration, and a warm, celebratory handoff reinforce the customer's satisfaction and make them feel valued. This is also a perfect opportunity to go over service schedules and encourage the customer to return for maintenance needs.

- **Efficient Documentation**: Streamlining the paperwork process reduces wait times and enhances the overall buying experience. Digital signing options and prepared documents make for a quicker, more efficient close.

- **Follow-up for Loyalty**: Sending a thank-you message a few days after the purchase shows the dealership's commitment to long-term satisfaction. This can also open the door for referrals and positive reviews.

2.5. Post-Purchase and Ownership

Even after the sale, the customer remains a valuable connection. I've seen that a good post-purchase experience often results in future business, whether through maintenance visits, trade-ins, or referrals. The relationship doesn't end when they drive off the lot—in fact, it's just beginning. Today, dealerships have the tools to stay connected, offering everything from maintenance reminders to loyalty rewards, ensuring that customers think of them first when it's time to buy again.

Dealership Opportunity:

- **Service Reminders**: Timely reminders for maintenance services, like oil changes or tire rotations, reinforce the dealership as a go-to service provider.

- **Loyalty Programs**: Incentives for repeat purchases or service visits encourage customers to stay connected.

- **Follow-up for Feedback and Referrals**: Asking for feedback, while offering help with any post-purchase questions, creates a lasting positive impression and helps generate referrals or repeat business.

Conclusion:

By reflecting on how the buying cycle has evolved, we gain a clearer perspective on how to meet modern customers' needs. Where once the focus was on face-to-face interactions at each dealership visit, today it's about fostering an online presence, providing prompt virtual support, and delivering a memorable, efficient in-store experience that complements the research customers have already done. This shift demands a mix of digital and in-person engagement that meets customers at each phase, from initial curiosity to long-term ownership satisfaction.

Section 3. Buyer Motivations and Concerns When Calling or Inquiring Online

In today's market, the motivations and concerns driving customers to reach out to a dealership are as diverse as their individual circumstances. When a buyer calls or inquires online, they're typically motivated by a specific need, question, or concern they've encountered during the research phase. Understanding these underlying motivations and addressing concerns with clarity and empathy can make the difference between a lost lead and a scheduled appointment.

Unlike the traditional "lot visit" of the past, where buyers could freely browse and ask questions in person, online inquiries and calls are opportunities for dealerships to provide the insight and assurance buyers need to feel confident moving forward. Here, we explore some common motivations and concerns behind customer inquiries and how dealerships can respond effectively.

3.1. Motivations Behind Buyer Inquiries

Chapter II

a. Gathering Specific Information

- **Motivation**: Often, a buyer inquires because they need precise information that isn't fully addressed online. This might include vehicle availability, specific feature details, or clarification on listed prices and promotions. While they may be close to deciding on a particular vehicle, they need additional information to solidify their choice.

- **Dealership Response**: Provide clear, concise answers that demonstrate your knowledge and transparency. A prompt, informed response shows that the dealership values the customer's time and is ready to help them make a well-informed decision.

b. Verifying Availability and Condition

- **Motivation**: With the high turnover of inventory in most dealerships, buyers want reassurance that the car they're interested in is still available and in the condition advertised. Many buyers are hesitant to visit in person unless they feel confident that their preferred vehicle is on-site and ready for inspection.

- **Dealership Response**: Confirm availability promptly and offer to set up an appointment for the customer to view or test drive the vehicle. Statements like, "Yes, that model is available, and we'd be happy to have it prepped for a test drive at your convenience," give buyers a sense of assurance and personalized service.

c. Comparing Options and Pricing

- **Motivation**: Today's buyers are meticulous about comparing options. They'll often reach out to inquire about incentives, financing rates, or package options to assess where they can find the best value. This may also include questions about trade-in values and discounts.

- **Dealership Response**: Respond with transparency and detail. It's important to provide enough information to position the dealership as competitive without overwhelming the customer. Offering to schedule a time to discuss financing, trade-ins, or exclusive offers in person can help keep the conversation moving toward a showroom visit.

d. Seeking Assurance of a Fair Deal

- **Motivation**: Many buyers inquire to ensure they're getting a fair deal, especially if they've had previous negative experiences or if they're wary of aggressive sales tactics. They might be cautious of hidden fees, confusing terms, or "too good to be true" promotions.

- **Dealership Response**: Emphasize transparency, fairness, and honesty in your communication. Reassure them that the dealership is committed to clarity and is ready to walk through any details with them. Using phrases like, "We believe in full transparency, and I'd be happy to break down the costs with you," can build trust and put their concerns at ease.

e. Convenience and Efficiency

- **Motivation**: For many customers, the online inquiry is a way to save time. They want to have as many questions answered as possible before committing to an in-person visit. This motivation is particularly common among busy professionals and those who are far from the dealership.

- **Dealership Response**: Respect their time by responding quickly and providing succinct, useful information. Let them know that by setting an appointment, they can get a dedicated time slot to see the car, ask questions, and finalize details without waiting. Offering an online appointment scheduling option can also streamline the process.

3.2. Common Buyer Concerns and How to Address Them

Understanding the main concerns customers have when reaching out—whether by phone or online—is essential for overcoming hesitations that could delay or prevent a visit. By addressing these concerns proactively, dealerships can create a reassuring experience that builds confidence and encourages in-person interaction.

a. Concern: Pressure to Commit or Buy

- **Buyer's Perspective**: Many customers fear being pressured into making decisions before they're ready, based on experiences with aggressive sales tactics. This fear often makes buyers hesitant to engage, as they worry about being pushed to commit over the phone or in their first visit.

- **Dealership Response**: Reassure the customer that there's no pressure to buy. Use language that promotes a comfortable, low-pressure experience, such as, "We're here to answer your questions and help you make the best decision—no rush, no pressure." Reinforcing this message shows that the dealership prioritizes customer needs over sales targets.

b. Concern: Fear of Hidden Costs or Fees

- **Buyer's Perspective**: Hidden costs or unclear pricing is a top concern for many car shoppers. They may be apprehensive about fees not listed in the advertised price or additional costs that could arise unexpectedly during the purchase.

- **Dealership Response**: Address this concern head-on by emphasizing transparent pricing and willingness to go over all costs. A statement like, "We list our prices with transparency and are happy to review any fees with you in detail," can dispel worries about hidden costs and promote trust in the dealership.

c. Concern: Vehicle Condition or Quality

- **Buyer's Perspective**: Particularly for used cars, customers may worry about the vehicle's condition and whether it matches the online description. They may fear that there could be issues that aren't disclosed upfront.

- **Dealership Response**: If a customer inquires about a specific vehicle, take the opportunity to confirm its condition, possibly including a brief description of its inspection process or any certification that comes with it. Offering a test drive or an appointment to see the car in person and highlighting any pre-sale inspection standards reinforces confidence in the vehicle's quality.

d. Concern: Lack of Clarity on Financing and Trade-In Values

- **Buyer's Perspective**: Financing can be one of the more intimidating aspects of the car-buying process. Buyers often have questions about down payments, loan terms, and interest rates, as well as uncertainties around trade-in values.

- **Dealership Response**: Offer an overview of the financing options available and assure them that an in-person visit would allow them to work with a financing specialist. Statements like, "We can discuss financing options in detail and review your trade-in value at the dealership to make sure you get the best offer," help make the dealership seem approachable and supportive.

e. Concern: Quality of Customer Service and Follow-Up

- **Buyer's Perspective**: Some buyers, particularly those with previous negative experiences, worry about the level of customer service they'll receive. They might be concerned that they won't receive personalized attention or that the dealership won't follow up on their needs.

- **Dealership Response**: Demonstrate responsiveness and reliability in your initial interactions by responding promptly and personally to inquiries. If they have a specific question, take the time to follow up with a thorough answer. A statement like, "Our priority is your satisfaction, and I'll be here to help every step of the way," signals that their experience matters and sets the tone for a positive relationship.

Conclusion

Understanding customer motivations and concerns is vital for any dealership's inbound strategy. By addressing these motivations and easing common concerns with empathy, clarity, and honesty, dealerships can build trust and encourage customers to take the next step. In the end, each inquiry represents not just a potential sale but an opportunity to make a lasting impression that keeps customers coming back—and brings them into the dealership with confidence.

4. Addressing the Competitive Nature of Dealership Shopping and Creating Urgency

The automotive sales industry is highly competitive, with buyers today having more options than ever before. Online research tools, third-party listing sites, and readily accessible dealer reviews make it easy for customers to compare prices, inventory, and customer experiences across multiple dealerships. This transparency empowers buyers but also heightens competition, as dealerships must work harder to stand out. Creating a sense of urgency can make the difference in whether a customer decides to visit your dealership or continue their search elsewhere.

4.1. Recognizing the Competitive Landscape

Car buyers today can access a wealth of information within minutes, narrowing down options from dozens of dealerships to a handful based on factors like pricing, reputation, and availability. This shift has redefined dealership shopping, turning it into a largely digital process where buyers "visit" multiple dealerships online before they even set foot on a lot. Understanding this shift is essential to crafting a sales approach that stands out in an increasingly competitive environment.

Key Factors Driving Competition:

- **Pricing Transparency**: Customers can easily compare pricing between dealerships, with sites like CarGurus and Edmunds giving them insight into average market values and "fair price" indicators.

- **Availability of Inventory**: With online inventory listings, customers can see which dealerships have their preferred make, model, and trim level without ever leaving their homes.

- **Dealership Reviews and Ratings**: Third-party review sites, like Google Reviews and DealerRater, empower buyers to assess a dealership's customer experience before making contact, making reputation a critical factor in their decision-making.

Given these factors, it's crucial to offer potential buyers a clear reason to choose your dealership over competitors—and to convey that the time to act is now.

4.2. Strategies for Differentiation and Creating Urgency

Creating urgency in a competitive environment means giving customers a reason to act quickly, without making them feel pressured. It's about emphasizing the unique value your dealership offers, as well as gently highlighting the risks of waiting too long to make a decision.

a. Limited Availability and Inventory Scarcity

In many cases, customers may delay decisions if they believe that a vehicle will be available later or that they have time to weigh options. However, pointing out limited availability can encourage them to act sooner.

- **Communicate Scarcity with Transparency**: Mentioning that a particular model or trim level is in high demand or that inventory is moving quickly can gently nudge buyers to prioritize their decision. Statements like, "This model has been very popular, and we've had a lot of inquiries about it recently," or "We currently have just a few in stock, and they're selling fast," create awareness of demand without sounding overly pushy.

- **Highlight Seasonal or Model-Year Considerations**: Customers may be motivated by the awareness that certain models or incentives are only available for a limited time. Mentioning an upcoming model-year changeover or end-of-season incentives can help create a natural urgency around current inventory.

b. Exclusive Offers and Time-Sensitive Incentives

Offering time-sensitive incentives, such as a weekend sale, trade-in bonuses, or finance rate reductions, can set your dealership apart and encourage customers to take prompt action.

- **Use Limited-Time Incentives**: Promotions that are only available for a set period, such as holiday sales events or end-of-month bonuses, create urgency by adding a deadline. When buyers know an offer won't last, they're more inclined to prioritize visiting the dealership. Phrasing like, "We're running this promotion through the end of the week," or, "This rate is only available until the end of the month," lets them know they should act soon to benefit.

- **Personalized Incentives for In-Person Visits**: Offering exclusive bonuses for customers who come in for a test drive or appraisal within a certain timeframe can be particularly effective. For example, "If you can come in this week, we're offering an additional trade-in incentive that could increase your trade value," is a powerful way to combine urgency with tangible benefits.

c. Showcase the Customer Experience and Relationship Focus

Customers are more likely to choose a dealership where they feel valued and respected, particularly if they sense that the dealership is focused on building a relationship rather than just making a sale. Demonstrating this relationship-first approach can differentiate your dealership in a way that resonates with buyers who may feel wary of high-pressure sales tactics.

- **Emphasize Personalization and Customer Care**: Let buyers know that your goal is to help them find the best fit for their needs, not simply to make a sale. Statements like, "We want to make sure this car is right for you," or, "We're here to answer any questions and help you feel confident in your decision," show that their satisfaction is your priority.

- **Offer a Hassle-Free Test Drive Experience**: Many customers are concerned about the time commitment involved in visiting a dealership. By highlighting a seamless, no-pressure test drive process—such as having the car prepped and ready at a designated time—you can set your dealership apart as a customer-centered option.

d. Communicate Market Trends and Resale Value Considerations

Many buyers are motivated by the potential resale value of their purchase or concerns about future price trends. By sharing market insights, you can give customers a reason to consider making a decision sooner rather than later.

- **Highlight the Investment Potential**: Let customers know if certain models are holding their value exceptionally well or if market trends indicate that prices may increase in the near future. For example, "This model has one of the highest resale values in its class," or, "We're seeing market prices increase on this model due to high demand," can appeal to the customer's practical concerns.

- **Educate on Interest Rate Fluctuations**: If interest rates are rising, informing customers of the potential financial benefits of locking in current rates can be a powerful motivator. Phrasing like, "We're expecting interest rates to go up soon, so now is a great time to secure financing on this model," can create urgency around financing opportunities.

4.3. Avoiding Overly Aggressive Urgency Tactics

While urgency can be effective, it's important to approach it with balance and authenticity. Buyers can sense when urgency is artificial or forced, and overly aggressive tactics can lead to resistance or even mistrust. The goal is to create urgency that feels natural, emphasizing the benefits of acting sooner rather than later.

Key Practices to Avoid:

- **Avoid Overusing Pressure Language**: Phrases like "Act now before it's gone!" or "This deal won't last!" may feel too forceful for today's more cautious and research-focused buyers. Instead, focus on providing helpful information that encourages them to act based on genuine benefits.

- **Respect the Customer's Timeline**: If a customer expresses hesitation or a need to think things over, avoid repeated attempts to pressure them. Instead, reiterate your availability to answer questions or provide additional information whenever they're ready.

4.4. Reinforcing Urgency with Follow-Up Communication

Once urgency is established, timely follow-up communication can reinforce the message and keep your dealership top-of-mind. Strategic, respectful follow-up serves as a gentle reminder of the benefits you've highlighted and helps customers remember their initial motivation for reaching out.

Effective Follow-Up Strategies:

- **Reminder Emails or Texts About Inventory and Promotions**: A friendly message that reiterates the customer's interest and reminds them of the vehicle's popularity or limited availability can help sustain urgency without seeming pushy.

- **Follow-Up on Incentive Expiration**: If an incentive is about to expire, a courteous reminder that highlights the benefit (e.g., lower financing rate, trade-in bonus) may prompt action. For instance, "I just wanted to remind you that our trade-in bonus runs through the end of the month. Let us know if you'd like to take advantage of it!"

- **Offer Additional Assistance or Information**: If the customer seems undecided, offer to provide further information or answer any additional questions they may have. A message like, "I'd be happy to provide more details on financing options or available features to help you decide," reinforces that the dealership is there to assist, not pressure.

Conclusion:

In a highly competitive dealership environment, creating urgency thoughtfully and genuinely is essential. By understanding the motivations behind a customer's hesitation and gently guiding them toward timely action, dealerships can create a sense of priority without resorting to hard-sell tactics. Whether through highlighting inventory scarcity, offering limited-time incentives, or personalizing the buying experience, creating urgency in a customer-centered way encourages engagement and increases the likelihood of a dealership visit.

Chapter III

Energizing Your Call Performance for Maximum Impact

The tone, energy, and approach used on each call can significantly influence the customer's impression of the dealership. To make each call count, there are key techniques that sales and BDC reps can use to optimize energy, boost confidence, and maximize engagement.

Section 1. Get in the Zone: Preparing Physically and Mentally
The first step to effective calling is setting up an environment that enables confidence, positivity, and connection with customers. Just as athletes follow a warm-up routine to optimize performance, sales representatives benefit from physical and mental preparation to convey energy, enthusiasm, and professionalism over the phone.

1.1 Stand and Move Freely

Using a headset allows you to move naturally, a key part of maintaining energy and control during calls. Standing rather than sitting has several advantages:

- **Increased Vocal Strength**: When you stand, your voice projects more clearly and confidently. Standing up opens the diaphragm, allowing for fuller, more dynamic breathing, which gives your voice a strong, resonant quality that commands attention.

- **Natural Hand Gestures**: Physical movement while speaking naturally enhances your tone, enthusiasm, and expressiveness, which customers can hear and feel, even if they can't see you. When your hands are free to gesture, it prevents your tone from sounding too stiff or robotic, helping you create a more engaging experience for the listener.

- **Boosted Energy**: Movement helps combat the potential monotony of back-to-back calls. With the freedom to move, you can release energy physically, which keeps you fresh and motivated.

Chapter III

If your workspace allows, you may consider setting up a standing desk or an adjustable desk converter. This can encourage a more active, dynamic stance throughout your calling session, promoting consistent energy.

1.2 Smile and Engage Your Body Language

Smiling while talking has a powerful effect on your voice, instantly making you sound friendlier and more approachable. Smiling helps create a warm, welcoming tone, establishing rapport and making customers feel comfortable and valued. Here's how to make the most of your body language, even when the customer can't see you:

- **Mirror In-Person Gestures**: Act as if the customer is right in front of you. Smiling, nodding, and expressing engagement physically translates into a more pleasant tone. These subtle changes make a noticeable difference in how receptive customers feel, setting the foundation for a positive interaction.

- **The "Mirror Effect"**: Smiling and projecting warmth can encourage the customer to mirror your positive energy, even over the phone. Studies have shown that mirroring is an effective rapport-building tool, so smiling and engaging your body language increases the chances that customers will respond in a similarly positive tone.

- **Mental Preparation**: Before the call, try visualizing a friendly face to help establish a smile and positive body language naturally. This small mental shift can set the tone for a positive call and remind you to bring energy and warmth.

If you're not used to smiling while on the phone, practice with a mirror nearby to observe the subtle impact it has on your tone and energy.

1.3 Know Your Scripts and Be Ready to Respond

Preparation goes a long way toward sounding polished, confident, and professional on every call. Thoroughly knowing your scripts ensures that you're prepared to respond seamlessly to customer questions, objections, and comments, without sounding overly rehearsed or mechanical. Here's how to ensure smooth, natural communication:

- **Memorize Key Phrases**: While improvisation is often necessary, knowing key parts of your script by heart gives you confidence in the flow of the call. This frees you up to focus on the conversation rather than scrambling for the right words.

- **Practice Adaptability**: Familiarity with scripts allows you to pivot naturally if the conversation shifts direction. This adaptability can make you sound like you're having a real conversation rather than reading from a script, which customers tend to respond to more positively.

- **Personalize Where Possible**: While scripts are necessary for structure, remember to personalize the call when possible. Customers appreciate hearing their name and knowing that they're more than just a sales target. This touch of personalization adds to the rapport you're building, making each call feel unique.

Practice your scripts out loud before your shift begins, focusing on clarity, confidence, and smooth transitions. If you record these practice sessions, you'll be able to fine-tune your tone and pacing, helping you sound more polished and prepared.

Conclusion: Final Thoughts on Getting in the Zone

Creating the right environment and preparing physically and mentally can make a dramatic difference in call performance. A prepared, energized, and confident rep not only sounds more compelling but also enhances customer experience, setting the stage for a positive conversation. By optimizing your physical stance, body language, and mental readiness, you'll be fully equipped to engage each customer and make every call as impactful as possible.

Section 2. Energize with Music

Adding music to your routine is a simple yet effective way to boost your energy and enthusiasm on calls. Upbeat music has the power to shift your mood, giving you a more positive, engaging tone that customers can hear—even though they can't see you. I've found that **upbeat instrumental music**, like house or electronic tracks without lyrics, helps to keep my energy high without causing distraction. Lyrics in songs can sometimes interfere with concentration, especially during conversations where you need to listen and respond attentively.

Recommended Playlists

I put some playlists of upbeat music that you may enjoy on my YouTube channels. You can find these playlists here on YouTube:

> https://www.youtube.com/@ChristopherJCunningham

2.1 Practical Ways to Play Music While on Calls

If you're using a headset connected to your computer, you can easily incorporate background music from your computer while making calls. Here's a quick guide to make sure you're set up to keep the music in your ears—at just the right volume.

Computer   **Setup**
Many modern headsets connected to computers have audio controls that allow you to adjust the volume balance between your calls and the background music. Here's how:

Chapter III

- **Adjust Volume Levels**: Start playing your music on YouTube, Spotify, or directly from MP3 files. Set the music volume to a low level so it provides an upbeat background without overpowering the customer's voice. Adjust the headset's volume so you can still hear the caller clearly.
- **Create Custom Playlists**: If you're using a music service, consider creating playlists that loop or shuffle through high-energy tracks, so you don't have to interrupt your flow to switch songs.

Phone Setup with Earbuds

If your headset is not connected to a computer, you can still enjoy music during calls by using a simple workaround. Place an earbud from your phone inside the ear cushions of your telephone headset. This technique provides the music without interfering with your ability to hear the customer. Just make sure the music volume is low enough to avoid drowning out any part of the conversation.

- **Layering Sound**: Place one earbud from your phone in one ear, and your call headset over both ears. Adjust the volume on your phone to the point where you can hear the music softly but are still fully aware of the customer's voice.

Old-School Techniques for High Energy

Back in the '90s, when I first discovered the benefits of music on calls, I used a telephone headset with large ear cushions and layered in the earphones from my Sony Walkman cassette player. Later, I upgraded to a CD player, and then eventually to an MP3 player as technology progressed. I even did this on my motorcycle rides, tucking my earbuds under my helmet for a private soundtrack on the go. This same technique works just as well in a sales environment, where listening to energizing music can set you apart from colleagues who might look and sound drained. While they may be counting down the hours, you'll be *smiling and dialing*, *moving and grooving*, and bringing high energy into every interaction.

2.2. Why It Works: The Positive Impact on Mood and Performance

The combination of upbeat music and a physical, active posture can have a measurable impact on your performance. Music keeps your mood elevated, making it easier to handle the repetitive nature of call work and helping you maintain a fresh, positive tone with each customer. Customers respond well to energy and enthusiasm; it gives the impression of confidence, knowledge, and a genuine interest in their needs.

As a bonus, your music routine can become a morale booster, giving you something enjoyable to look forward to each time you pick up the phone. Your energy won't just be noticeable to customers, it will set you apart in the workplace as well, showing your team that you bring a positive approach to every call.

Conclusion:

By incorporating music into your call routine, you can infuse energy into your voice, stand out in your customer interactions, and set the tone for a productive, enjoyable workday. When it comes to making calls, there's no substitute for enthusiasm, and music is a powerful tool to keep that enthusiasm high, one track at a time.

Section 3. The Power of Mirroring: Building Rapport with Customers

Mirroring is a powerful communication technique that involves subtly reflecting the tone, pace, and language of the person you're speaking with. When used effectively, mirroring helps build rapport, trust, and a sense of understanding between you and the customer. In a sales environment, especially over the phone, mirroring can make the customer feel more comfortable and connected, increasing the likelihood that they will be receptive to your offer.

3.1. Matching Tone and Energy

One of the first things to observe in a call is the customer's tone and energy level. Mirroring these elements can make the conversation feel more natural and comfortable for the customer.

- **Assess the Customer's Energy**
  If a customer sounds excited and energetic, reflect that energy back with a warm, enthusiastic tone. Conversely, if a customer speaks slowly or has a calm demeanor, slightly lower your own energy to match theirs. This shows that you're in tune with their mood and makes them feel heard and understood.

- **Use Subtle Adjustments**
  Mirroring doesn't mean copying the customer exactly. It's about subtle adjustments to your own style to align with theirs, creating a harmonious interaction. Just a slight change in energy level or tone can help establish a stronger connection without feeling artificial or forced.

3.2. Pacing the Conversation
The speed at which people speak is often a reflection of their personality and current state of mind. Mirroring the pace of the conversation can make the customer feel like you're on the same wavelength.

- **Adjust Your Speaking Speed**
  If the customer speaks quickly, try to match their pace. This helps maintain the flow of the conversation and shows that you can keep up with them. For customers who speak slowly, slow down your speech slightly to match their rhythm, creating a more relaxed and accommodating atmosphere.

- **Pause When They Pause**
  Pacing also includes the use of pauses. If the customer pauses frequently to think, allow for those pauses rather than rushing in to fill the silence. This

helps avoid interrupting their thought process and allows them the space to process the information or questions you're sharing.

3.3. Language and Phrasing

Another effective aspect of mirroring is using similar language, phrasing, or even keywords that the customer uses. This can make the conversation feel more relatable and personalized.

- **Reflect Key Words and Phrases**
  Listen for specific terms or phrases the customer uses to describe what they're looking for or their needs, such as "budget-friendly," "family vehicle," or "reliable." By incorporating these terms in your responses, you show that you're listening and adapting your responses to fit their perspective.

- **Match Formality or Casualness**
  If a customer is formal and direct, mirror that level of professionalism in your responses. For more casual customers, you can adopt a slightly more relaxed tone to make the conversation feel friendlier. Be sure to maintain professionalism but adjust the level of formality to match the customer's comfort zone.

3.4. Benefits of Mirroring in Sales Calls

Mirroring not only helps establish trust but also has a persuasive effect on the customer. When you mirror a customer's tone, energy, and pace, they often end up mirroring you in return. This dynamic works in your favor by subtly influencing them to adopt your level of enthusiasm, focus, and confidence.

- **Increased Customer Comfort and Engagement**
  Mirroring creates a subconscious connection, helping customers feel at ease and more open to conversation. When customers feel understood, they're more likely to stay engaged and become more receptive to your suggestions. Over time, they may begin to reflect your own confidence and enthusiasm, making them more likely to respond positively to an appointment invitation.

- **Enhanced Persuasion Through Mutual Mirroring**
  When customers begin to mirror you, it signifies alignment and agreement. As you project confidence, excitement about the vehicle, and a strong sense of urgency, they may start adopting that same tone and urgency. This alignment helps nudge them toward making a decision, increasing the likelihood they'll commit to visiting the dealership.

- **Boosted Trust and Credibility**
  Mirroring positions you as relatable and credible in the customer's eyes, which builds trust and makes them more inclined to see you as a partner in their car-buying journey. By maintaining a steady, confident tone, you set a

reassuring pace that the customer can follow, creating a smoother path to booking the appointment.

Final Note on Mirroring and Persuasion

Mirroring isn't just a technique for connection; it's also a tool for persuasion. When done effectively, it encourages customers to align with your energy, enthusiasm, and confidence, helping them see the dealership visit as the natural next step. By mastering this subtle yet powerful approach, you make each call more engaging and more persuasive, bringing customers one step closer to a sale.

Practical Tips for Mirroring in Your Calls

To incorporate mirroring effectively, remember that subtlety is key. Overdoing it can come across as insincere or forced. Practice listening closely to each customer, making small adjustments in your tone, pace, and language that feel natural within the conversation.

- **Practice with Colleagues**: Try practicing mirroring techniques with colleagues or in mock calls to become comfortable with adjusting your style in real time.
- **Listen Before Mirroring**: Take a few seconds to listen actively before making adjustments to ensure you're mirroring appropriately.
- **Be Authentic**: Authenticity is crucial. Use mirroring as a tool to enhance connection, not as a tactic to manipulate the conversation.

Conclusion: Mirroring as a Tool for Connection

Mirroring is a subtle yet effective way to make each customer interaction feel personal and genuine. By adjusting your tone, pacing, and language to align with the customer, you're creating a rapport that can make a significant difference in the success of the call. Customers are more likely to book appointments with someone they feel understands them, and mirroring is a powerful way to create that sense of connection and trust.

Incorporate mirroring as part of your call routine, and watch how it elevates your engagement with customers, leading to higher appointment rates and a more enjoyable experience on both ends of the call.

Section 4. Track Your Own Performance and Build Consistency

Beyond mindset and technique, tracking performance metrics on calls helps you understand what's working and where there's room for improvement.

- **Set Personal Benchmarks**
  Aim to measure your call success rate (appointments set, customer engagement) against dealership standards, and track your progress over time. These benchmarks help establish consistency and set realistic goals for improvement.

- **Self-Review and Adjust**
  If your CRM or calling system allows call recording, take the time to review a few calls each week. Listening to your own calls can provide invaluable insights into your tone, timing, and effectiveness in handling objections or setting appointments. Take notes on areas where you can improve, such as clarity, engagement, or script adherence.

- **Seek Feedback and Refine Techniques**
  Don't hesitate to ask for feedback from managers or peers on your calling technique. External perspectives can reveal things you might not notice yourself, such as your pace, clarity, or overall tone. Use this feedback to refine your approach, adding elements that enhance the customer experience.

Conclusion: Elevate Every Call with Energy and Professionalism

Every call represents an opportunity to connect with a potential customer, and it's crucial to bring your best self to each interaction. By creating a positive physical environment, adding motivating music, approaching calls with preparation and energy, and mirroring the customers, you'll build a consistent, professional call routine that makes a difference. Combined with tracking your performance, these techniques help you optimize each conversation, create lasting impressions, and bring more customers into the dealership. With each call, you're not only setting appointments but also setting the stage for successful sales and long-term customer relationships.

Chapter IV

Appointment Setting Techniques

Section 1. Initial Approach – Engaging the Customer from the Start

When a customer reaches out to the dealership, they've already taken a significant step toward making a purchase decision. Whether they're calling about a specific vehicle or submitting an inquiry online, their interest is a golden opportunity. The initial approach you take with these customers sets the tone for the entire interaction and can make the difference between an appointment scheduled and a lead lost. In this section, we'll cover how to confidently engage the customer right from the start, focusing on establishing trust, demonstrating professionalism, and leading them toward scheduling an in-person visit.

1.1. Welcome the Customer with Enthusiasm and Confidence

Your tone of voice is crucial when connecting with a potential buyer. Customers should feel they're speaking with someone who is friendly, knowledgeable, and ready to help. Begin with a warm greeting that projects enthusiasm, instilling confidence from the moment they hear your voice.

- **Example**: "Hi, thanks for calling! This is [Your Name] at [Dealership Name], and I'm excited to help you today. Who do I have the pleasure of speaking with?"

- **Tip**: Use positive language and avoid sounding rushed. Your enthusiasm will make the customer feel welcomed and valued.

1.2. Listen Actively and Answer Questions Briefly

When customers reach out, they may have specific questions about a vehicle's availability, features, or price. While it's essential to provide them with clear answers, remember that your primary goal is not to give away all the details but to guide them toward an in-person visit where they can see the vehicle for themselves.

- **Answer Directly**: Address their questions with brief, direct answers that satisfy their initial curiosity without overwhelming them with details.

- **Redirect to Appointment Setting**: After addressing their inquiry, smoothly transition the conversation toward setting an appointment by highlighting the advantages of seeing the vehicle in person.

- **Example**:
    - Customer: "Is the [Vehicle Model] still available?"
    - You: "Yes, we still have it, and it's priced to sell quickly. Let's set up a time for you to come in and check it out. Would this afternoon at 3:45 or tomorrow morning at 10:15 work for you?"

1.3. Establish Yourself as a Helpful and Knowledgeable Resource

Customers respond well to representatives who sound knowledgeable and ready to assist. Make it clear through your approach that you're the right person to help them find exactly what they're looking for.

Avoid Hard Sales: This initial call is not the time to push a sale but to provide a friendly, welcoming experience.

1.4. Acknowledge Their Time and Schedule Constraints

Customers appreciate when you respect their time. By recognizing that they're busy, you position yourself as considerate and professional, making them more likely to want to engage with you further.

- **Use Assumptive Language**: Assume they're interested in coming in soon, as this creates a sense of importance around setting a specific time.

- **Offer Two Appointment Options**: Present two options for appointment times within the next 24 to 48 hours, giving them flexibility while subtly creating urgency.

- **Example**:
    - "I know your time is valuable, and I want to make this as convenient as possible for you. Would a 4:00 appointment today or a 10:00 slot tomorrow morning work better?"

1.5. Create a Sense of Urgency and Exclusivity

Customers are more likely to schedule an appointment when they feel that the vehicle they're interested in may not be available if they delay. By mentioning that there's high interest in the vehicle or limited availability, you create urgency without pressuring them.

- **Frame the Appointment as Valuable**: Convey the benefit of seeing the vehicle in person sooner rather than later.

- **Mention Interest or Availability**: Highlight that the vehicle may not last long in the current market, especially if the customer is calling near the weekend or a holiday.

- **Example**:
    - "This [Vehicle Model] has been popular lately, and it's unlikely to be here through the weekend. Let's get you in to see it as soon as possible—would this afternoon or tomorrow morning work better for you?"

Conclusion: The Power of a Strong Initial Approach
The first impression you make sets the foundation for a successful appointment. By engaging the customer with enthusiasm, answering their questions briefly, and guiding them toward an appointment, you establish yourself as a helpful resource they can trust. This initial approach doesn't just secure a scheduled time; it builds rapport and creates a sense of importance around the appointment. When customers feel welcomed and valued, they're more likely to follow through, show up, and ultimately make a purchase.

Section 2. Establishing Control – Propose Specific Times

Setting an appointment isn't just about securing a time on the calendar; it's about guiding the customer toward a decision with confidence and control. When you take charge of the conversation by proposing specific appointment times, you subtly lead the customer toward an outcome that is in both their best interest and the dealership's. This approach allows you to establish yourself as a knowledgeable advisor while maintaining momentum and ensuring the customer's intent to visit the dealership remains strong. Let's explore how to structure this part of the call for maximum effectiveness.

2.1. Avoid Open-Ended Questions and Take Charge

When asking the customer for a specific appointment time, avoid questions that are too open-ended. Open-ended questions—such as "When would you like to come in?"—put the decision entirely in the customer's hands, which may lead to indecision or delays.

- **Example of What to Avoid**: "When would you like to come in?"
- **Better Approach**: "I have a couple of times available today and tomorrow. Let's find one that works for you."

By taking the lead, you reinforce the importance of the appointment and convey confidence that visiting the dealership is the best next step.

2.2. Offer Two Specific Times to Choose From

Chapter IV

Presenting two specific appointment times within the next 24 to 48 hours adds structure to the conversation and creates a sense of urgency. This technique, known as the "either-or" choice, is highly effective in maintaining control of the interaction, as it minimizes the chance of a noncommittal response from the customer.

- **Example**:
    - "I have a 3:45 this afternoon or an 11:15 tomorrow morning available. Which one works better for you?"

By limiting their choices to two specific times, you subtly push the customer toward committing to one of the options, keeping the conversation on track.

2.3. Leverage Urgency by Offering Appointments Within 24–48 Hours

Timing matters when it comes to setting appointments. Scheduling the visit within the next day or two maximizes the chance that the customer's excitement remains high and reduces the risk of them visiting another dealership first. Urgency is particularly effective when paired with subtle hints about the vehicle's popularity or limited availability.

- **For Example**:
    - "This model has been getting a lot of interest, and we've already had several inquiries today. Let's get you in to see it soon. Would this afternoon or tomorrow morning work better?"

If the customer insists on an appointment further out, gently remind them that vehicles sell quickly and that seeing it soon can help them avoid missing out.

2.4. Use Odd Appointment Times for a Professional Touch

Offering appointment times at slightly off-hour intervals (e.g., 3:45 instead of 4:00) adds a layer of professionalism and suggests a structured schedule, reinforcing the idea that appointments are limited and valuable.

- **Example**: "I have a 3:45 slot today or a 10:15 tomorrow morning—either of those work for you?"

This technique subtly communicates that the dealership is busy, making the appointment feel more exclusive and reinforcing urgency.

2.5. Stay in Control with Confident Language

Confident language instills trust and minimizes hesitation from the customer. Use direct statements rather than questions to convey that you're knowledgeable and have their best interests in mind.

- **Examples of Confident Language**:
    - "Let's get you in to see it this afternoon or tomorrow morning."

Chapter IV

> o "I'll hold that spot for you today at 2:15 or tomorrow at 11:00. Which works best?"

Confident phrasing like this eliminates uncertainty, demonstrating that you're in control and ensuring the customer feels that visiting the dealership is the natural next step.

2.6. Confirm the Appointment with a Strong Close

Once the customer has chosen a time, restate the appointment details clearly to reinforce the commitment and confirm their intent to show up. Providing these details at the close of the conversation further solidifies the appointment, reducing the chances of a no-show.

- **Example**:
  - "Great, so we'll see you tomorrow at 11:15. I'll have the [Vehicle Model] ready for you, and we'll get you right into a test drive when you arrive. If anything changes on your end, just give me a call."

Concluding with a clear, concise summary of the time, date, and vehicle ensures that the customer feels committed to the appointment, minimizing the risk of last-minute cancellations.

Conclusion: Taking Charge to Drive Results

The "either-or" method of proposing specific appointment times is a proven way to establish control, build urgency, and secure customer commitment. By avoiding open-ended questions, using confident language, and reinforcing the appointment details, you create a seamless and structured experience that guides the customer toward an in-person visit. Mastering this technique allows you to consistently turn inquiries into showroom visits, paving the way for increased sales and a stronger customer connection.

Section 3: Scripts for Common Scenarios

When customers reach out to the dealership, they often have specific questions about vehicle availability, pricing, features, or trade-in options. These inquiries provide an excellent opportunity to engage them and, ultimately, schedule an appointment. Using well-crafted scripts helps ensure consistency, professionalism, and a smooth transition to an in-person visit. Here are effective scripts for some of the most frequent scenarios encountered in appointment setting.

3.1. Easy phone scripts that work for various scenarios

Scenario 1: Availability Check

Customer Question: "Is this vehicle still available?"

Chapter IV

Objective: Confirm availability and create urgency for an in-person visit.

Script:
- **You**: "I know we've had a lot of inquiries about that model recently, and I believe someone was just in looking at it. Let me check on its availability for you. Could I get your name and number in case we get disconnected?"
- *(Pause for 10-15 seconds)*
- **You**: "Yes, it looks like we do still have it, but at this price, it probably won't last through the weekend. I can get you in for a test drive this afternoon. I have a 3:45 available, or tomorrow at 11:15. Which works best for you?"

Key Points:
- Briefly hold the customer to check availability (even if you already know), adding a layer of authenticity.
- Use specific appointment times to guide the customer toward an immediate decision.

Scenario 2: Price Inquiry

Customer Question: "What's your best price on this vehicle?" or "Is that the best price you can do?"

Objective: Acknowledge the question while reinforcing the value of an in-person visit and the vehicle's competitive pricing.

Script:
- **You**: "Great question! You probably noticed that our inventory is competitively priced to sell quickly, and we don't mark up just to bring the price back down. This vehicle is priced to move, and with the interest we've had, it likely won't make it through the weekend. Let's get you in to see it. I have an opening at 2:30 this afternoon, or tomorrow morning at 9:45. Which works better?"

Key Points:
- Reinforce that the price is already competitive to deter further negotiation over the phone.
- Offer immediate appointment times to maintain control and emphasize urgency.

Scenario 3: Feature Inquiry

Customer Question: "Does the vehicle have [specific feature]?" (e.g., leather seats, sunroof, third-row seating)

Objective: Confirm the feature, highlight the vehicle's popularity, and guide the customer to an in-person visit.

Chapter IV

Script:
- **You**: "Yes, that model does have [feature], and it's been a popular choice because of it. Let's set a time for you to see it up close. Are you available this afternoon at 4:15, or would tomorrow morning at 10:30 work better for you?"

Key Points:
- Confirm the feature confidently, underscoring the vehicle's desirability.
- Immediately pivot to setting an appointment, assuming the customer's interest remains strong.

Scenario 4: Trade-In Valuation Request

Customer Question: "How much can I get for my vehicle as a trade-in?"

Objective: Set an in-person appraisal, emphasizing the advantage of an on-site evaluation for an accurate offer.

Script:
- **You**: "Great question! Our appraiser can give you the best value with an in-person evaluation. I have appraisal times open this afternoon at 3:15 or tomorrow at 11:30. Which one works best for you?"

Key Points:
- Emphasize that an on-site appraisal is necessary for an accurate valuation.
- Directly offer specific appointment times to create an efficient transition toward an in-person visit.

Scenario 5: Outbound Call to Internet Inquiry (No Question Asked)

Objective: Take control by setting an appointment without waiting for customer-led questions.

Script:
- **You**: "Hi [Customer's Name], this is [Your Name] from [Dealership]. Did I catch you at a good time?"
- *(Pause briefly, then proceed regardless of their response)*
- **You**: "I'm reaching out to help schedule your test drive for the [Vehicle Model] you showed interest in. I have availability this afternoon at 3:45 or tomorrow at 10:15. Which works better?"

Key Points:
- Start with a polite intro, then lead straight into appointment options.
- Avoid lengthy explanations or waiting for the customer to ask additional questions, keeping the focus on setting the appointment.

Chapter IV

Scenario 6: Outbound Call for Trade-In Inquiry (Customer Wants to Know Trade-In Value)

Objective: Set an appraisal appointment with the appraiser to maximize trade-in value.

Script:
- **You**: "Hi [Customer's Name], this is [Your Name] from [Dealership]. Did I catch you at a good time?"
- *(Pause briefly, then continue)*
- **You**: "I see you're interested in trading in your [Current Vehicle Model]. To ensure we give you the most accurate value, our appraiser would need to see it in person. I have an appointment available at 2:15 today or tomorrow at 11:00. Which one works for you?"

Key Points:
- Make it clear that the appraisal requires an in-person visit.
- Offer specific times, allowing the customer to commit to a concrete schedule.

3.2. Solidifying the appointment.

Setting an appointment means nothing if the customer does not show up. The second half of your appointment setting script solidifies the appointment to maximize your show rate.

Script:
"Do you have a pen or pencil and something to write with?"

"OK write 123-456-2782, that's my direct number, and then write Chris Cunningham, and write 123 Main St., Anytown, North Carolina, that's our address, and write 2:15 today. I'll have that Mercedes gassed up, and parked out front so that when you arrive we can get you right into your test drive." If anything comes up with that vehicle, I'll be sure to give you a call, and if anything comes up on your end, please give me a call at my direct number. Fair enough? Great, I'll see you at 2:15 then."

Now if they don't have access to a pen or pencil, maybe they're driving let them know that you will text them the information.

"Can I text you my name, direct number, and our address? Great, I'll have that Mercedes gassed up, and parked out front so that when you arrive we can get you right into your test drive." If anything comes up with that vehicle, I'll be sure to give you a call, and if anything comes up on your end, please give me a call at my direct number. Fair enough? Great, I'll see you at 2:15 then."

Key Points:

- Gain commitment from the customer to show up. They understand that you will be waiting on them and will have their vehicle of interest parked in front of the store for them to drive.

Conclusion: Consistency and Confidence in Each Interaction

Scripts provide a foundation for consistent, effective communication across different scenarios, ensuring that customers receive a seamless experience regardless of their initial inquiry. By following these scripts, you maintain control, demonstrate professionalism, and create a clear path for the customer to visit the dealership. Practice these responses to become comfortable with each scenario, so you can adapt to customers' needs while keeping the focus on securing an in-person appointment.

Section 4. Confirming Appointments, Reminders, & Reschedules

Securing an appointment is a significant first step, but ensuring that customers actually show up is equally critical. A well-structured confirmation process helps reinforce the commitment, builds anticipation, and reduces the likelihood of last-minute cancellations. This section outlines effective techniques for confirming appointments, using personalized reminders, professional follow-ups, and solidifying details to maximize show rates.

4.1. Recap the Appointment Details at the End of the Call

The first confirmation step happens immediately after setting the appointment. Before ending the initial call, provide the customer with a quick summary of the appointment details. This recap solidifies their commitment and clarifies any potential misunderstandings about the time, date, or purpose of the appointment.

4.2. Send a Personalized Email Confirmation

Immediately after the call, follow up with an email that includes the appointment details, dealership location, and your contact information. The email serves as a written record and a quick reference for the customer, ensuring they have all the necessary information.

Template:
Subject Line: "Your Appointment Confirmation for [Vehicle Model] at [Dealership]"

Body:
"Hi [Customer's Name], Thank you for scheduling an appointment to see the [Vehicle Model]. Here are the details:
Date and Time: [Appointment Date and Time]
Location: [Dealership Address]

Chapter IV

Contact: [Your Contact Number] I'll have the vehicle ready for you upon arrival, and if anything changes, please don't hesitate to reach out. Looking forward to seeing you then!
Best,
[Your Name, Dealership Name]"

Key Points:
- Make the email concise and professional.
- Restate the appointment details and provide location information.
- Include your contact information for any last-minute changes.

4.3. Send a Text Message Reminder

As the appointment time approaches, a quick text reminder is an effective way to reconfirm the appointment. Send the reminder a few hours before the appointment or, if it's the following day, send it on the morning of the appointment. Texts are direct, immediate, and often viewed more quickly than emails, making them ideal for last-minute reminders.

Script:
"Hi [Customer's Name], this is [Your Name] from [Dealership]. Just a reminder that we're all set to meet at [Appointment Time] today to go over the [Vehicle Model]. We're looking forward to seeing you! Let me know if there's anything you need before you arrive."

Key Points:
- Keep the message short and friendly.
- Reinforce the anticipation of seeing the vehicle in person.
- Include your name and dealership to make the reminder feel personal.

4.4. Make a Confirmation Call on the Day of the Appointment

For appointments set a day or two in advance, a same-day confirmation call is highly effective for reinforcing the commitment. This quick check-in reassures the customer that their visit is a priority and gives them an opportunity to confirm any last-minute details. Use a friendly, confident tone, and keep the call brief.

Script:
"Hi [Customer's Name], this is [Your Name] from [Dealership]. I'm just calling to let you know we have the [Vehicle Model] gassed up and ready for you. We're looking forward to seeing you at [Appointment Time]. Will you still be able to make it?"

Key Points:
- Mention that the vehicle is prepared for them, adding a personal touch.
- Confirm the appointment time, creating a sense of accountability.
- Ask if they're still able to make it, reinforcing the commitment.

4.5. Provide Location Details and Directions if Needed

If the customer is unfamiliar with the dealership's location, consider including directions or a quick link to a map in your email or text message reminders. This simple addition removes any last-minute barriers to attendance and shows attention to detail.

Example:
"Our address is [Dealership Address], and you can find directions here: [Google Maps Link]. Just let me know if you need help finding us."

Key Points:
- Include a map link for easy access.
- Avoid overly detailed directions unless the customer specifically requests it.

4.6. Handle Last-Minute Cancellations with Flexibility

If a customer calls to cancel or reschedule close to the appointment time, handle it professionally and offer alternative appointment times. Flexibility and understanding in these moments can help salvage the appointment and demonstrate a commitment to their needs.

Script:
"I completely understand, [Customer's Name]. Let's reschedule at a time that's more convenient for you. I have an opening at [Alternative Time] tomorrow or [Another Time] later this week. Which one works best?"

Key Points:
- Acknowledge the cancellation politely.
- Offer alternative times to keep the appointment on the books.
- Be flexible to accommodate their schedule.

Conclusion: The Power of a Confirmed Appointment

Confirming appointments through multiple touchpoints—verbal, email, text, and same-day calls—helps ensure that customers feel valued, informed, and excited about their visit. Each confirmation step reinforces the commitment, reducing the chances of no-shows and making it more likely that the customer will arrive prepared to see and test drive the vehicle. Mastering these confirmation techniques can make a significant difference in show rates, ultimately contributing to more sales and higher customer satisfaction.

Chapter V

Handling Objections and Delays

Section 1. Scripts for Overcoming Common Objections (e.g., Best Price, Trade-In Value)

Objections around price, trade-in value, or specific features are common in the car sales process. While these questions can feel like barriers, they're often opportunities to build trust and strengthen the customer's interest in visiting the dealership. By handling objections professionally and confidently, you can turn potential resistance into motivation for an in-person visit. Here are scripts and strategies for addressing some of the most frequent objections you'll encounter.

Objection 1: "Is that your best price?" or "Can you go any lower?"

Objective: Acknowledge the customer's concern, emphasize the vehicle's value, and create urgency for an in-person visit to discuss further details.

- **Script**:
  - **You**: "Great question! We price our inventory very competitively so you can feel confident that you're getting a fair deal without needing to haggle. Each vehicle is priced to sell quickly based on market demand, and this particular model has been very popular. I'd recommend seeing it in person to understand all the features it offers."
  - **Transition to Appointment**: "I'd love to show you the vehicle and go over the details in person. Would today at 3:15 or tomorrow at 10:45 work better for you?"

- **Key Points**:
  - Emphasize that the price is already competitive.
  - Avoid negotiating over the phone, as the goal is to have them see the vehicle in person.
  - Use urgency to encourage a prompt visit to the dealership.

Objection 2: "How much will you give me for my trade-in?"

Objective: Emphasize that an accurate trade-in value can only be determined in person, while creating anticipation around the appraisal process.

Script:
- **You**: "We'd be glad to appraise your vehicle and ensure you get the best value. However, to give you an accurate offer, our appraiser would need to see it in person, check the condition, and assess it based on current market rates. This way, you know you're getting the maximum value possible."
- **Transition to Appointment**: "I have a few appraisal appointments open today at 4:15 and tomorrow morning at 10:00. Which one works best for you?"

Key Points:
- Reinforce that the best way to ensure a fair value is with an in-person assessment.
- Avoid discussing trade-in values over the phone, keeping the focus on setting an appraisal appointment.
- Offer specific appointment times to keep the conversation on track.

Objection 3: "I want to compare with other dealerships first."

Objective: Respect the customer's intent to shop around, but highlight the unique qualities of the dealership or the vehicle and why it's worth visiting sooner rather than later.

Script:
- **You**: "I completely understand. Many of our customers compare options before making a final decision. What we often hear is that, after seeing the quality of our inventory and the value we offer, they feel confident about their choice. Plus, I'd hate for you to miss out if this vehicle sells in the meantime."
- **Transition to Appointment**: "Why don't you come in today at 3:45 or tomorrow at 11:00 to see it for yourself? If you still want to look around afterward, you'll have all the information you need to make the best choice."

Key Points:
- Show understanding of the customer's position without dismissing their intent to compare.
- Highlight your dealership's unique offerings and the vehicle's appeal.
- Use urgency to encourage a prompt visit, as availability may be limited.

Objection 4: "I need to talk to my spouse/partner first."

Objective: Respect the customer's need to consult with their partner, but offer a time for both to come in to see the vehicle, facilitating the decision-making process together.

Script:
- **You**: "I completely understand! A purchase like this is definitely something to discuss with your partner. Many of our customers find it helpful to bring

Chapter V

their spouse along so they can see the vehicle in person and go over everything together."

- **Transition to Appointment**: "I have availability for both of you to come in this afternoon at 4:15 or tomorrow morning at 10:30. That way, you can see it firsthand and make the decision together. Which time works better?"

Key Points:
- Show respect for the customer's decision to involve their spouse or partner.
- Suggest bringing their partner to the appointment, making it a joint experience.
- Offer specific times for them both to visit, keeping the appointment a priority.

Objection 5: "Can you send me more details by email?"

Objective: Agree to send limited information while emphasizing the benefit of seeing the vehicle in person. This approach respects the customer's need for information without giving everything away online.

Script:
- **You**: "Absolutely, I can send you a quick summary with some key highlights. But to get a full sense of the vehicle's condition and all the features, I highly recommend seeing it in person. Photos and descriptions are great, but there's nothing like sitting in it and experiencing it for yourself."

- **Transition to Appointment**: "Why don't we set up a time for you to come by and take a closer look? I have a spot at 2:45 this afternoon or tomorrow at 9:30. Which one works for you?"

Key Points:
- Agree to send limited details to build trust while keeping the focus on the in-person experience.
- Emphasize the benefits of a personal visit to fully appreciate the vehicle.
- Offer two specific times to keep control of the conversation and guide the customer toward a decision.

Objection 6: "I don't have time to come in right now."

Objective: Respect the customer's busy schedule while creating urgency and offering flexible times for an appointment.

Script:
- **You**: "I understand! We work with many customers who have tight schedules, and I'm happy to be flexible with you. This vehicle has been getting a lot of attention, so I'd hate for you to miss out if it sells before you're able to see it."

- **Transition to Appointment**: "I have a few openings later this week if that would work better. Would [Date and Time] or [Another Date and Time] fit into your schedule?"

Key Points:
- Show understanding of the customer's limited time, offering flexibility in scheduling.
- Reinforce the importance of the appointment by highlighting the vehicle's popularity.
- Provide multiple options to accommodate their schedule while keeping the focus on getting them to the dealership.

Conclusion: Turning Objections into Opportunities

Handling objections professionally and confidently can turn potential barriers into reasons for customers to visit the dealership. By validating their concerns, emphasizing the benefits of an in-person experience, and guiding the conversation toward specific appointment times, you maintain control and keep the appointment as the primary goal. Each of these scripts provides a structured yet flexible approach to address objections and keep the conversation moving forward.

Section 2. Strategies for Creating Urgency Around Limited Inventory or High Demand

Creating a sense of urgency can be a powerful tool in encouraging customers to visit the dealership sooner rather than later. When customers understand that vehicles are in high demand or that inventory is limited, they're more likely to prioritize an in-person visit to avoid missing out on the car they want. This section provides actionable strategies for building urgency in a natural, customer-centric way, emphasizing the value of acting quickly without coming across as pushy.

2.1. Highlight Popularity and Recent Interest in the Vehicle

One effective way to build urgency is by mentioning the vehicle's popularity and recent inquiries from other customers. This creates a subtle form of social proof—when customers see that others are interested, they're more likely to perceive the vehicle as desirable and act quickly.

Script:
- "I've had a lot of interest in this [Vehicle Model] recently. In fact, we had a few calls and inquiries about it today. Given the demand, I'd hate for you to miss out, so let's set up a time to see it soon."
- Appointment Transition: "I have an opening at 2:30 this afternoon or 10:45 tomorrow. Which time works better for you?"

Key Points:
- Mentioning recent interest adds credibility to the urgency.

Chapter V

- Keep the tone conversational to avoid sounding forced or exaggerated.

2.2. Leverage Limited Inventory with Transparency

Customers often understand that high-demand vehicles have limited availability, especially if they're looking at popular models or trims. By framing limited inventory as a practical reality, you communicate honesty and encourage customers to visit sooner.

Script:
- "This model has been moving quickly, and we only have a couple left in stock. Because they're so popular, I wouldn't want you to miss the chance to see it."
- Appointment Transition: "Would today at 3:15 work, or would tomorrow at 11:00 be better?"

Key Points:
- Use specific language like "only a couple left" or "limited stock" to create a sense of scarcity.
- Maintain transparency, so the customer feels you're prioritizing their needs rather than using a sales tactic.

2.3. Emphasize Upcoming High-Traffic Days (Weekends or Sales Events)

If the vehicle's availability coincides with an upcoming high-traffic day, like a weekend or dealership sales event, use this to your advantage. Suggest that visiting before these busy times will give the customer a better opportunity to view the vehicle without competition.

Script:
- "We have a big sales event this weekend, and this model has already been getting a lot of attention. If you'd like to avoid the rush, I'd recommend coming in before the weekend so we can give you a more personal look at it."
- Appointment Transition: "I have an opening tomorrow at 10:30 or this afternoon at 4:00. Which works best?"

Key Points:
- Use upcoming high-traffic times as an incentive for early visits.
- Position the visit as an opportunity to avoid competing interest.

2.4. Mention Market Demand for Specific Features or Trim Levels

For vehicles with unique features or trims that are particularly popular, highlight this demand to encourage a quick decision. Customers looking for specific attributes may act more promptly if they understand that availability is limited.

Script:

- "This [specific trim or feature] has been very popular. We only get a few with these specs, and they usually sell fast. I'd love for you to come see it while it's still available."
- Appointment Transition: "I can reserve a time for you today at 3:45 or tomorrow at 9:15. Which would be better for you?"

Key Points:
- Use specific details about the trim or features to create a more tailored sense of urgency.
- Frame the visit as a valuable opportunity to see something rare.

2.5. Reinforce Value for Money by Mentioning the Competitive Price

When a vehicle is priced competitively, emphasizing its value can reinforce urgency. Customers may perceive limited-time pricing as an incentive to visit the dealership sooner.

Script:
- "This model is priced very competitively, and we've had inquiries from multiple people looking for this deal. I want to make sure you have the chance to see it before it's gone."
- Appointment Transition: "Could you come by this afternoon around 2:15, or would tomorrow at 10:30 work better?"

Key Points:
- Emphasize that the competitive price adds urgency without using high-pressure language.
- Reinforce that a quick visit helps them make the most of this limited pricing.

2.6. Remind Customers of Limited Seasonal Inventory (for Seasonal or New Models)

For seasonal vehicles (like SUVs in winter or convertibles in summer) or new models that may have just launched, remind customers that these vehicles are limited. Customers seeking specific types of vehicles may be more motivated to visit sooner if they understand that seasonality affects availability.

Script:
- "Since it's the beginning of [season] and [Vehicle Model] is very popular, we expect to sell through quickly. I'd recommend coming in soon to see it before we're limited on options."
- Appointment Transition: "How about this afternoon at 3:00 or tomorrow morning at 11:00?"

Key Points:
- Use seasonality to increase the urgency, especially for vehicles that are in demand based on the time of year.

Chapter V

- Position the visit as a timely decision for customers interested in seasonally relevant models.

Conclusion: Building Urgency with Confidence

Creating urgency around limited inventory or high demand helps customers understand the value of acting quickly. By highlighting recent interest, limited stock, or seasonal availability, you offer them a practical reason to prioritize a visit to the dealership. Each of these strategies reinforces the importance of seeing the vehicle in person, fostering a sense of urgency that feels natural and encouraging without being overly forceful.

Mastering these strategies can help you not only increase in-person appointments but also build a positive reputation for honesty and transparency, enhancing the overall customer experience.

Section 3. Techniques for Maintaining Control When Customers Try to Extend the Timeline

In the car sales process, it's common for customers to hesitate, delay their decision, or push the appointment further into the future. While their reasons may vary, the key to maintaining momentum is to keep control of the conversation, respectfully address their concerns, and guide them toward a timely visit. Here, we'll explore effective techniques to handle delays while keeping the interaction focused on achieving a quick and committed appointment.

3.1. Acknowledge the Customer's Concern with Empathy

When a customer expresses hesitation or suggests pushing the appointment out, acknowledge their concern with understanding. Showing empathy builds trust and gives you a foundation to gently redirect the conversation toward an earlier visit.

> **Script**:
> **Customer**: "I'd like to come in next week instead."
> - **You**: "I completely understand! It sounds like you have a busy schedule, and I want to make this as convenient as possible. We've had a lot of interest in this model recently, though, so I'd hate for you to miss out. Let's see if we can find a time that works this week."
>
> **Key Points**:
> - Validate their schedule or concerns to make them feel heard.
> - Quickly pivot back to scheduling within a shorter timeframe, highlighting recent interest in the vehicle.

3.2. Use Urgency to Reinforce the Value of a Timely Visit

Highlighting the potential scarcity of the vehicle or its high demand can make customers rethink delaying their visit. By conveying that time is of the essence, you create a sense of priority around the appointment.

Script:
"I understand! This [Vehicle Model] has been very popular, and I wouldn't want you to miss the chance to see it while it's still available. I could hold a spot for you tomorrow at 3:15 or Friday morning at 11:00. Does one of those times work?"

Key Points:
- Emphasize limited availability or popularity to add urgency.
- Provide two near-term options to keep the conversation focused on a prompt visit.

3.3. Present the Appointment as a Low-Commitment Opportunity

If the customer feels pressured, they may try to delay because they're not yet committed to purchasing. Position the appointment as an opportunity to explore the vehicle with no pressure to buy, which can help reduce their resistance to visiting sooner.

Script:
- "I completely understand if you're still considering your options. This appointment is just an opportunity to see the [Vehicle Model] and get any questions answered. No pressure at all. I'd recommend coming by sooner so you can keep your options open. How does tomorrow at 2:45 sound?"

Key Points:
- Remove any pressure or commitment to make the appointment feel less formal.
- Offer a short-term option to gently encourage a timely visit.

3.4. Position Yourself as a Resource to Address Any Immediate Concerns

When customers attempt to delay because they're unsure or have questions, take the opportunity to act as a knowledgeable resource who can help them make an informed decision. This encourages them to visit sooner to receive answers and clarity.

Script:
- "I completely understand if you're weighing all your options. I'd be happy to answer any questions you might have or address any concerns in person to make things clearer. How about coming in tomorrow at 2:30 or Friday morning at 11:15?"

Key Points:
- Offer to address their concerns in person, helping to resolve their hesitation.
- Provide short-term options, positioning yourself as a trusted advisor.

Chapter V

3.5. Set a Tentative Appointment with Flexibility

If the customer insists on a later date, suggest a tentative appointment with flexibility to adjust as needed. This helps secure a spot while keeping the door open for a potentially sooner visit.

Script:
- "If you'd prefer next week, we can tentatively set a time for then, and if anything opens up sooner, I'd be happy to adjust it for you. How about Tuesday at 11:00?"

Key Points:
- Create a sense of commitment by setting a tentative appointment.
- Leave room for flexibility, subtly encouraging an earlier visit if possible.

3.6. Remind Them of the Benefits of a Quick Visit

When customers delay because they feel uncertain, remind them of the value of seeing the vehicle in person and experiencing it firsthand. Reframe the visit as an essential part of the decision-making process, rather than a high-pressure appointment.

Script:
- "Seeing the [Vehicle Model] in person and taking it for a test drive really helps in making a confident decision. I wouldn't want you to miss out on that experience. Could we plan for tomorrow at 4:00 or Saturday morning at 9:45?"

Key Points:
- Emphasize the importance of an in-person visit to aid decision-making.
- Encourage a short-term appointment that aligns with their interest in making the best choice.

Conclusion: Staying in Control with Confidence and Flexibility

Handling timeline delays requires a balance of empathy, urgency, and proactive guidance. By acknowledging the customer's needs while maintaining control of the conversation, you can encourage them to prioritize a timely visit to the dealership. Each of these strategies helps build urgency, reinforce the value of the appointment, and keep the process moving forward without feeling pushy or inflexible. Mastering these techniques allows you to lead the interaction with confidence, fostering a positive experience that encourages the customer to act sooner.

Chapter VI

Confirming Appointments and Maximizing Show Rates

Section 1. Confirming Appointments with Multi-Touch Reminders

Setting an appointment is just the first step; ensuring that customers show up is where the real opportunity lies. A multi-touch reminder strategy increases the likelihood of customers attending their scheduled appointment by creating consistent, friendly reminders across different channels. This layered approach includes a combination of confirmation calls, emails, text messages, and day-of reminders, each designed to reinforce the appointment in a professional, non-intrusive way. Here's how to structure an effective multi-touch reminder strategy.

1.1. Immediate Email Confirmation

After scheduling the appointment, send an email confirmation as soon as possible. This written reminder provides the customer with essential details, acts as a reference for the appointment, and gives you an opportunity to showcase your professionalism. The email should be concise, friendly, and include the dealership's contact information and address.

>   **Email Template**:
>   **Subject**: "Your Appointment Confirmation for [Vehicle Model] at [Dealership]"
>   **Body**:
>   "Hello [Customer's Name], Thank you for scheduling an appointment to see the [Vehicle Model]. Here are the details:
>   **Date and Time**: [Appointment Date and Time]
>   **Location**: [Dealership Address]
>   **Contact**: [Your Contact Number] I look forward to helping you explore your options. Please feel free to reach out if you have any questions or need to reschedule.
>   Best regards,
>   [Your Name, Dealership Name]"
>
>   **Key Points**:

Chapter VI

- Include all key details in the body of the email, so the customer has the information at their fingertips.
- Use a friendly, professional tone that reinforces the importance of the appointment.

1.2. Text Message Reminder One Day Before the Appointment

Text messages are direct, timely, and often viewed more quickly than emails, making them ideal for reminding customers one day before the appointment. The message should be short, reinforcing the appointment's details and giving the customer an easy way to confirm or reschedule.

Text Message Template:
"Hi [Customer's Name], this is [Your Name] from [Dealership]. Just a quick reminder of your appointment tomorrow at [Time] to see the [Vehicle Model]. Looking forward to helping you! Let me know if there's anything you need."

Key Points:
- Keep the message concise and friendly.
- Mention your name and dealership to personalize the interaction.
- Offer to assist if they have questions or need further help.

1.3. Confirmation Call the Morning of the Appointment

For appointments set in advance, a quick call on the morning of the appointment helps solidify the customer's commitment. This call should be brief and positive, reinforcing that the dealership is prepared and looking forward to their visit.

Script:
"Hello [Customer's Name], this is [Your Name] from [Dealership]. I'm just giving you a quick call to confirm that we'll see you at [Appointment Time] today. We have the [Vehicle Model] ready for you, and we're excited to help you explore it. If you have any questions or if anything changes, please feel free to reach me at this number."

Key Points:
- Keep the tone enthusiastic to create anticipation.
- Provide an easy way for them to contact you if their plans change.
- Reinforce that the vehicle is prepared for their arrival, adding a personal touch.

1.4. Same-Day Text Reminder, Sent a Few Hours Before the Appointment

A final text reminder sent a few hours before the appointment ensures that the customer doesn't forget and reinforces that the dealership is ready to assist them. This reminder should be quick, friendly, and respectful of the customer's time.

Text Message Template:

"Hi [Customer's Name], just a friendly reminder about your appointment at [Time] today to see the [Vehicle Model] at [Dealership]. If you have any questions or need directions, feel free to reply to this message. Looking forward to seeing you!"

Key Points:
- Keep it friendly and concise, reminding them of the time and dealership.
- Offer assistance if they need help finding the location or have other last-minute questions.
- Maintain a helpful, positive tone to minimize any sense of pressure.

1.5. Optional: Automated Email Follow-Up After the Appointment

If the appointment is scheduled for the end of the day or after hours, an automated email follow-up helps maintain professionalism if the customer couldn't attend or needs to reschedule. This follow-up email should be polite, offering to assist with another appointment at their convenience.

Email Template:
Subject: "Following Up on Your Appointment at [Dealership]"
Body:
"Hello [Customer's Name], We noticed you couldn't make it to your appointment today. We understand that schedules can change, and we'd be happy to help you find a new time to visit. Please let us know if there's anything we can do to assist.
Best,
[Your Name, Dealership Name]"

Key Points:
- Approach this follow-up with understanding, offering to accommodate their schedule.
- Keep it polite and inviting, letting them know that the dealership is ready to work with their availability.

Conclusion: Building Consistency and Connection with Multi-Touch Reminders

A multi-touch reminder approach increases appointment attendance rates by reinforcing the importance of the appointment at different points leading up to the scheduled time. Each touchpoint—whether by email, text, or call—reminds the customer of their commitment while making them feel valued and respected. By confirming with consistency and a friendly tone, you create a positive experience from the start, encouraging customers to follow through with their visit. Mastering this process helps you build trust, manage customer expectations, and maximize the likelihood of a successful in-person meeting.

Section 2. Sending Email, Text, and Call Confirmations

Chapter VI

In today's busy world, customers often need reminders to stay on top of their commitments, including appointments at the dealership. Effective communication across email, text, and phone calls helps keep customers engaged and reinforces their commitment to visit the dealership. By using multiple channels strategically, you increase the chances that customers remember the appointment, arrive on time, and feel valued by the dealership. Below are best practices for sending email, text, and call confirmations.

2.1. Email Confirmation: Providing a Detailed Record

An email confirmation is essential for offering customers a detailed record of the appointment, including date, time, location, and contact information. This first touchpoint sets a professional tone and provides a reference they can look back on, helping to reduce no-shows.

When to Send: Immediately after scheduling the appointment
Content to Include:
- Appointment date and time
- Dealership location with address
- Contact information for the salesperson or BDC representative
- Any additional details like parking information or special instructions

Sample Email Template:
Subject: "Your Appointment Confirmation for [Vehicle Model] at [Dealership]"
Body:
"Hello [Customer's Name], Thank you for scheduling an appointment to view the [Vehicle Model] with us! Here are the details for your upcoming visit:
Date and Time: [Appointment Date and Time]
Location: [Dealership Address]
Contact: [Your Contact Number] We look forward to helping you find your ideal vehicle! If you have any questions or need to make changes, feel free to reach out.
Best,
[Your Name, Dealership Name]"

Key Points:
- Keep the email concise, friendly, and professional.
- Highlight the dealership's contact details to make it easy for customers to reach out if needed.
- Include a polite call to action encouraging them to reach out with questions or to reschedule if necessary.

2.2. Text Confirmation: A Quick and Direct Reminder

Chapter VI

Text messages are ideal for a short, direct reminder a day before the appointment. Customers tend to see and respond to texts quickly, making them highly effective for reinforcing the appointment details close to the scheduled time.

When to Send: One day before the appointment and again a few hours before on the day of the appointment

Content to Include:
- Friendly reminder of the appointment time
- Dealership name
- Contact information in case they have questions

Sample Text Template:
"Hi [Customer's Name], this is [Your Name] from [Dealership]. Just a reminder of your appointment tomorrow at [Appointment Time] to see the [Vehicle Model]. Please reply if you have any questions or need directions. Looking forward to helping you!"

Key Points:
- Keep the text short and friendly.
- Include the salesperson's or representative's name to make it personal.
- Offer to assist if they need directions or have questions, showing customer-focused service.

2.3. Confirmation Call: Reinforcing Commitment with a Personal Touch

A confirmation call on the day of the appointment adds a personal touch that strengthens the customer's commitment. It's an opportunity to make a connection, answer any questions, and ensure the customer has everything they need for their visit. Calls also allow you to assess their intent and handle any potential cancellations proactively.

When to Call: The morning of the appointment or a few hours prior
Content to Include:
- Friendly reminder of the appointment time
- Confirmation that the vehicle is ready for them
- An invitation to call if they need help or have questions

Sample Call Script:
"Hello [Customer's Name], this is [Your Name] from [Dealership]. I'm just calling to confirm that we're all set to see you at [Appointment Time] today. I've made sure the [Vehicle Model] is ready for you, and we're looking forward to helping you. Please feel free to call me directly at this number if you have any questions or if anything changes."

Key Points:
- Keep the tone positive and enthusiastic to reinforce the value of the appointment.

- Reconfirm the time, adding a personal assurance that everything is ready for them.
- Offer to assist if they have last-minute questions or need additional information.

2.4. Handling Responses and Cancellations

When customers respond to reminders—especially with cancellations or rescheduling requests—it's essential to handle these professionally and with flexibility. Offer alternative times if they can't make the original appointment and ensure that you maintain a positive and accommodating tone.

- **Sample Response for Rescheduling**:
"Thank you for letting us know! We're more than happy to reschedule. I have availability tomorrow at 2:00 or Friday morning at 10:15. Which would work better for you?"

- **Sample Response for Confirmations**:
"Great! We'll see you at [Appointment Time]. Let me know if there's anything specific you'd like to go over during your visit."

Key Points:
- Be accommodating and flexible to maintain a positive relationship.
- Offer options if they need to reschedule, keeping the appointment on the books.
- Reinforce the dealership's commitment to providing an excellent experience.

2.5. Best Practices for Effective Multi-Channel Reminders

- **Use a Friendly, Consistent Tone Across Channels**: Your tone should remain warm and professional across email, text, and call reminders, reinforcing the dealership's focus on customer service.

- **Adjust Frequency Based on Customer Preferences**: Some customers may prefer fewer reminders, while others appreciate the communication. If possible, ask about their preferred contact method during the initial scheduling.

- **Maintain Balance Between Helpful and Non-Intrusive**: Ensure each reminder has a clear purpose and avoid overwhelming the customer with too many messages or calls. Each touchpoint should feel purposeful, not repetitive.

Conclusion: Building a Reliable Confirmation Routine

Using a structured approach to confirm appointments through email, text, and calls creates a seamless and professional experience for customers. This multi-touch confirmation process helps reduce no-shows, reinforces commitment, and shows the customer that they are a priority. By balancing the timing, tone, and content of each reminder, you ensure that customers feel supported, valued, and motivated to attend their scheduled appointment.

Section 3. How to Respond to Last-Minute Cancellations

Last-minute cancellations are an inevitable part of the dealership experience, but how you handle them can make a significant difference in whether that customer eventually visits. A well-thought-out response not only preserves the customer relationship but also demonstrates flexibility, understanding, and a commitment to excellent service. This section provides strategies and scripts for managing last-minute cancellations, with a focus on rescheduling the appointment and maintaining a positive connection.

3.1. Respond with Understanding and Professionalism

When a customer calls or messages to cancel at the last minute, respond with empathy and professionalism. Acknowledging their situation sets a positive tone and keeps the interaction customer-friendly.

Script:
- "I completely understand! Things come up, and I appreciate you letting us know. We'd still love to help you find the right vehicle, so please feel free to reach out when it's convenient for you."

Key Points:
- Avoid showing frustration or disappointment, even if the cancellation is inconvenient.
- Keep your response short, polite, and understanding.
- Leave the door open for future contact, encouraging them to reach out when they're ready.

3.2. Offer Flexible Rescheduling Options

If the customer's reason for canceling isn't a major conflict (such as a schedule change), propose rescheduling in a way that feels flexible and accommodating. By suggesting a few different time options, you give them a clear pathway to keep the appointment on their schedule.

Script:
- "No problem at all, [Customer's Name]. I understand that things can change. I'd be happy to reserve another time that works better for you. I have openings tomorrow at 10:30 or later in the week. Would either of those work?"

Key Points:

Chapter VI

- Offer specific options, rather than leaving it entirely open-ended, to keep some control over the timeline.
- Present rescheduling as a helpful solution, showing you value their time and convenience.
- Make it easy for them to choose a new time, and emphasize flexibility to maintain rapport.

3.3. Provide an Incentive for Rescheduling Quickly

Sometimes, customers are on the fence about rescheduling. Offering a small incentive, like a free car wash or a gift card, can encourage them to set a new appointment date sooner. Incentives should be genuine and relevant to the customer's experience.

Script:
- "I completely understand, [Customer's Name]. If you're able to come by within the next few days, I'd be happy to arrange a free car wash for your vehicle as a thank you for your flexibility. How about this Friday at 3:00, or would Saturday morning be better?"

Key Points:
- Keep the incentive small and relevant, avoiding anything that feels too "salesy."
- Mention the incentive casually to avoid any pressure.
- Focus on making the new appointment beneficial and timely.

3.4. Confirm Their Interest and Reinforce the Value of Visiting

If the customer seems hesitant to reschedule, this may indicate they're reconsidering their interest. In these cases, reaffirm the value of their visit by subtly reminding them of the vehicle's features, availability, or current promotions. This can help re-establish their motivation to come in soon.

Script:
- "I completely understand. Just so you know, this [Vehicle Model] has been very popular, and we're here to help answer any questions or go over the options in person whenever it's convenient for you. We'd love to keep you updated if you'd like to reschedule soon."

Key Points:
- Reinforce why their visit would be worthwhile, but avoid sounding pushy.
- Mention specific aspects of the vehicle or service that might reignite their interest.
- Emphasize the value of the visit to subtly encourage a reschedule.

3.5. Follow Up with a Polite Text or Email After a Missed Appointment

If a customer cancels last-minute and doesn't reschedule, a follow-up text or email within a day or two serves as a gentle reminder that the dealership is still interested in helping them. This keeps the line of communication open and may prompt them to reach out when they're ready.

Sample Text:
"Hi [Customer's Name], this is [Your Name] from [Dealership]. Just wanted to follow up and let you know we're here to assist whenever you're ready to explore options for the [Vehicle Model]. Feel free to reach out if you'd like to reschedule!"

Sample Email:
Subject: "We're Here to Help When You're Ready"
Body:
"Hello [Customer's Name], We missed seeing you at your scheduled appointment and wanted to let you know that we're here to help whenever it's convenient for you. The [Vehicle Model] is still available, and we'd love to answer any questions you may have or reschedule at a time that works better for you.
Best,
[Your Name, Dealership Name]"

Key Points:
- Keep the message polite and welcoming, focusing on your availability to help.
- Avoid applying pressure; simply offer your assistance and express understanding.
- Maintain a friendly, service-oriented tone to encourage them to reach out on their own time.

3.6. Monitor Cancellations and Identify Trends

In addition to responding to cancellations, it's helpful to analyze if there are patterns. Are certain days, times, or types of appointments more prone to cancellations? Monitoring these trends helps refine your approach and allows for preventive measures, like scheduling confirmations at optimal times or setting appointment reminders tailored to customers' needs.

Key Points:
- Track cancellations in your CRM system and identify any recurring patterns.
- Use the data to adjust your scheduling strategy, such as avoiding back-to-back appointments or high-cancellation times.
- Make adjustments based on trends to minimize last-minute cancellations over time.

Conclusion: Turning Last-Minute Cancellations into Future Opportunities

Chapter VI

Handling last-minute cancellations professionally and with empathy leaves the door open for future engagement. By offering flexible rescheduling options, subtle incentives, and timely follow-up messages, you can turn cancellations into opportunities to strengthen the customer relationship. Mastering this response process not only helps retain potential sales but also builds a reputation for flexibility and excellent customer service, encouraging customers to stay engaged with the dealership.

Chapter VII

Follow-Up Strategies For No-Shows and Rescheduling

Section 1: Techniques to Re-Engage Customers Who Didn't Show Up

No-shows are a common occurrence in the dealership world. While a missed appointment may seem like a lost opportunity, it's actually a chance to reconnect with potential customers. By using thoughtful follow-up techniques, you can turn a no-show into a rescheduled visit and demonstrate the dealership's commitment to providing excellent service. Here are strategies to re-engage no-show customers effectively and encourage them to return for another appointment.

1.1. Follow Up Quickly with a Friendly, Non-Pressuring Message

Reaching out soon after the missed appointment shows the customer that their visit was a priority. However, it's essential to keep the tone light and friendly, without applying pressure. This lets the customer know you're available whenever they're ready, without making them feel guilty for not showing up.

Script:
"Hi [Customer's Name], this is [Your Name] from [Dealership]. I noticed we missed you at your appointment and just wanted to check in. Is there anything we can help with or reschedule at a time that works better for you?"

Key Points:
- Keep the message warm and understanding to reduce any discomfort they may feel about missing the appointment.
- Avoid pressuring them to reschedule immediately; simply extend the offer for a new appointment.
- Send this message within a day of the missed appointment to ensure it feels timely and relevant.

1.2. Send a Reminder of the Vehicle's Unique Features or Availability

If the customer was interested in a specific vehicle, use the follow-up as an opportunity to remind them of what made that vehicle special. A quick message highlighting the car's features or limited availability can rekindle their interest and prompt them to reschedule.

Script:
"Hi [Customer's Name], just a quick note from [Dealership] about the [Vehicle Model] you were scheduled to see. This model has some amazing features, like [Feature 1, Feature 2], and it's been very popular lately. Let me know if you'd like to come by to check it out soon—I'd be happy to find a time that works for you."

Key Points:
- Mention specific features or unique selling points of the vehicle to reignite interest.
- Keep the tone helpful and enthusiastic, focusing on the value of the vehicle rather than the missed appointment.
- Emphasize that the vehicle is still available, subtly encouraging them to act before it's sold.

1.3. Offer a New Appointment with Added Convenience or Flexibility

If the original appointment time may have been inconvenient, offering added flexibility or alternative time options can make it easier for the customer to say yes to a new appointment. Suggesting specific, varied times shows that you're willing to work around their schedule.

Script:
"Hi [Customer's Name], I understand things get busy! If it's easier, I'd be happy to find a time that works better for you to come in and see the [Vehicle Model]. I have availability on [Day and Time] or [Alternative Day and Time]. Let me know if either works, or I'd be happy to work with your schedule!"

Key Points:
- Offer flexible options, making it easier for them to commit.
- Include varied times to give them more control over the scheduling.
- Keep the tone friendly and accommodating, showing you're willing to prioritize their convenience.

1.4. Mention a Small Incentive for Rescheduling Soon

To encourage a prompt return, offer a small, relevant incentive for rescheduling within the next few days. This can be something like a free car wash, a discount on services, or a gift card. The incentive should be genuine and help them see the added value of coming in sooner.

Script:
"Hi [Customer's Name], we'd still love for you to see the [Vehicle Model]. If you're able to reschedule for this week, I'd be happy to set you up with a complimentary car wash as a thank you for coming in. Does [Day and Time] or [Alternative Day and Time] work for you?"

Key Points:
- Offer a small, low-cost incentive to encourage a quick reschedule.
- Mention the incentive casually to avoid making it feel like a high-pressure tactic.
- Reinforce the positive experience they'll have by returning to the dealership.

1.5. Use a "Just Checking In" Email or Text if They Haven't Responded

If the customer hasn't responded to previous follow-up attempts, send a simple "just checking in" message. This friendly, unobtrusive approach keeps the conversation open without pressuring them. It serves as a polite reminder that the dealership is still available to help whenever they're ready.

Script:
"Hi [Customer's Name], this is [Your Name] from [Dealership]. I just wanted to check in and see if you're still interested in coming by to look at the [Vehicle Model]. No rush—just let me know if there's anything I can do to help!"

Key Points:
- Keep the tone friendly and light, showing patience and understanding.
- Avoid pushing for an immediate response; simply reopen the conversation.
- Offer to help with anything they might need to avoid further delays.

1.6. Send a Helpful Resource or Update Related to Their Interest

If possible, follow up by sharing a helpful resource related to their interests, like a link to a blog post on buying tips, a video on the specific vehicle model, or a current dealership promotion. Providing valuable content positions you as a helpful resource and keeps the dealership top-of-mind.

Script:
"Hi [Customer's Name], I thought you might find this interesting—[brief description of resource, like a blog post or video on the vehicle]. If you'd like to reschedule to take a closer look, just let me know. We're here to help whenever you're ready!"

Key Points:
- Share information that's genuinely relevant and beneficial.
- Use this message to stay connected without directly pressing for a reschedule.
- Keep it casual and service-oriented, showing the dealership's commitment to helping them make an informed decision.

1.7. Give One Last Friendly Follow-Up Call Before Closing the Loop

Chapter VII

If the customer remains unresponsive, a final follow-up call is a good way to close the loop while leaving the door open for future contact. Let them know they're welcome to reconnect whenever they're ready, and offer your direct contact information.

Script:
"Hi [Customer's Name], it's [Your Name] from [Dealership]. I just wanted to check in one last time about your appointment to see the [Vehicle Model]. We'd still be happy to work with your schedule and find a time that's convenient for you. Feel free to reach me directly at this number if you'd like to come by!"

Key Points:
- Keep the tone warm, polite, and leave the door open for future contact.
- Offer your direct number to make it easy for them to reconnect if they decide to revisit.
- This final follow-up closes the loop without applying pressure, leaving a positive impression of the dealership.

Conclusion: Turning No-Shows into Future Opportunities

By using thoughtful follow-up techniques, you can re-engage no-show customers and encourage them to reconsider a visit. Each of these approaches is designed to maintain a positive connection and gently encourage rescheduling without making the customer feel uncomfortable or pressured. By showing understanding, flexibility, and a commitment to service, you can turn a missed appointment into a renewed opportunity and leave a lasting impression that brings customers back when they're ready.

Section 2. Handling Rescheduling Requests Professionally

When customers request to reschedule, it's an opportunity to demonstrate flexibility, understanding, and commitment to excellent service. The goal is to make the process as easy as possible for the customer while still encouraging them to visit the dealership soon. By handling rescheduling requests professionally, you keep the customer engaged and committed to the appointment, reinforcing the dealership's dedication to customer satisfaction. Here are strategies and scripts for managing rescheduling requests gracefully and effectively.

2.1. Acknowledge the Customer's Schedule and Be Empathetic

When a customer asks to reschedule, acknowledge their need to change plans and respond with empathy. Showing understanding sets a positive tone and makes it easier for them to commit to a new date.

Script:
"Absolutely, [Customer's Name]! I completely understand—things come up all the time. Let's find a new time that's convenient for you."

Chapter VII

Key Points:
- Keep your response warm and understanding, making the customer feel at ease about the change.
- Avoid any tone of frustration; instead, approach the conversation with a helpful attitude.
- Reaffirm your commitment to helping them find a convenient time.

2.2. Offer Flexible Options with Specific Time Suggestions

Rather than leaving the new appointment time completely open-ended, offer two or three specific time options. This keeps the conversation focused on booking a new date and helps guide the customer toward committing to a specific time.

Script:
"No problem at all! I have an opening tomorrow at 3:00, Friday at 10:15, or Saturday at 11:30. Would any of these work for you?"

Key Points:
- Present two to three options, including different days and times, to make it easy for them to choose.
- Offering specific times prevents the conversation from dragging out and keeps control of the scheduling process.
- Ensure the options accommodate various schedules (morning, afternoon, and weekend).

2.3. Reassure Them That the Vehicle Will Be Ready and Waiting

If the customer is rescheduling to a different day, reassure them that the vehicle they're interested in will still be ready and waiting. This reminder shows that you're prioritizing their interests and keeping the vehicle available for them.

Script:
"No worries! I'll make sure the [Vehicle Model] is ready for you when you come in. We're here to help whenever you're ready to reschedule, so just let us know if there's anything specific you'd like to see or discuss when you arrive."

Key Points:
- Reinforce the dealership's commitment to keeping their vehicle of interest available and ready for them.
- This assurance adds a level of personal service and helps reduce their anxiety over the reschedule.
- Emphasize that the dealership is fully prepared for their visit to build excitement and commitment.

2.4. Confirm Their New Appointment with a Friendly Follow-Up

Chapter VII

Once the customer has selected a new time, confirm the details in a friendly follow-up email or text message. This written confirmation helps them remember the updated appointment and keeps the dealership top-of-mind.

Sample Text:
"Hi [Customer's Name], just confirming your new appointment time for [New Date and Time] to see the [Vehicle Model] at [Dealership]. Looking forward to helping you, and feel free to reach out if anything changes!"

Sample Email:
Subject: "Your Rescheduled Appointment Confirmation at [Dealership]"
Body: "Hello [Customer's Name], Thank you for rescheduling with us! Here's a quick confirmation of your new appointment time:
Date and Time: [New Date and Time]
Location: [Dealership Address] We're excited to see you and are here to answer any questions in the meantime.
Best,
[Your Name, Dealership Name]"

Key Points:
- Confirm the new date and time clearly to avoid confusion.
- Keep the message friendly and professional, expressing appreciation for their flexibility.
- Offer your contact information in case they need to make further changes.

2.5. If the Customer Wants to Reschedule Far Out, Encourage a Sooner Date

Sometimes, customers may try to push the appointment further out than necessary, which can increase the risk of a no-show or losing their interest. If this happens, suggest a sooner date, emphasizing flexibility to accommodate their availability.

Script:
- "I understand! Just to let you know, we're getting a lot of interest in the [Vehicle Model], so if you're able to come in this week, we'd love to prioritize your visit. Would [earlier date and time] work for you, or would [alternative sooner date and time] be better?"

Key Points:
- Keep the tone positive and friendly while gently suggesting an earlier date.
- Emphasize that the sooner date will ensure they don't miss out, especially if demand for the vehicle is high.
- Respect their time constraints while subtly encouraging a more immediate visit.

2.6. Offer a Quick Virtual Tour or Additional Information if They're Delaying Due to Uncertainty

If the customer is rescheduling due to hesitation or uncertainty about the vehicle, offer a virtual tour or share additional information to help them feel more confident in coming to the dealership.

Script:
- "If you'd like, I can send over a quick video tour of the [Vehicle Model] or answer any questions in advance. We're here to make the process as smooth as possible, and I'd love to help in any way that works best for you."

Key Points:
- Offering a video tour or pre-appointment information can help them feel more engaged.
- Use this opportunity to address any questions they may have that could prevent a future reschedule.
- Show that the dealership is proactive in supporting their decision-making process.

Conclusion: Ensuring a Positive Experience While Securing a New Appointment
Handling rescheduling requests professionally involves showing flexibility, empathy, and a commitment to customer satisfaction. By providing options, confirming their new appointment, and gently encouraging a sooner visit when possible, you maintain control of the scheduling process without pressuring the customer. These techniques foster a positive experience, helping the customer feel valued and supported while ensuring their continued engagement with the dealership.

Section 3. Scripts for Follow-Up Calls and Messages

Follow-up calls and messages are essential for keeping the customer engaged and moving them closer to an appointment or purchase. A well-crafted follow-up message reminds customers of their interest while addressing any hesitations they might have. Here are some effective scripts for different follow-up scenarios, designed to be friendly, professional, and persuasive.

3.1. Follow-Up Email for Unresponsive Leads

If a lead hasn't responded after the initial conversation, a follow-up email can re-engage them by subtly reminding them of their interest and reinforcing the vehicle's value. This approach works well for online inquiries or customers who initially showed interest but didn't schedule an appointment.

Email:
   Subject Line: "Still Interested in the [Vehicle Model]?"
   Body: "Hello [Customer's Name], I hope all is well! I wanted to follow up on your recent inquiry about the [Vehicle Model]. This is an excellent choice with [mention one or two key features or benefits]. We'd love to help you take a closer look and answer any questions you may have. If you're ready, I'd be happy to set up a quick test drive or virtual tour at a time that works

for you. Feel free to reply here or call/text me directly at [Your Phone Number].
Looking forward to helping you soon!
Best,
[Your Name, Dealership Name]"

Key Points:
- Highlight key features of the vehicle to renew their interest.
- Keep the tone helpful and professional without sounding overly eager.
- Offer flexible options for engagement (test drive or virtual tour) to make it convenient.

3.2. Follow-Up Call for Price or Feature Objections

If a customer hesitated over price or specific features, a follow-up call gives you a chance to address these objections. Emphasize the value and benefits that the vehicle offers to help them see it as a worthwhile investment.

Script:
- "Hi [Customer's Name], this is [Your Name] from [Dealership]. I know we talked about the pricing on the [Vehicle Model] last time, and I wanted to see if there's anything specific I can help with or clarify. I can go over any special financing options or trade-in benefits that might work for your budget. Would you like to come in and discuss this in person?"

Key Points:
- Address the customer's objection directly and offer solutions to help overcome it.
- Highlight financing or trade-in options to emphasize affordability.
- Use a welcoming tone to make them feel comfortable coming in to discuss further.

3.3. Text Message Reminder for Upcoming Appointment

Sending a reminder text ahead of an appointment can significantly reduce no-shows by keeping the appointment top-of-mind for the customer. This message should be brief, friendly, and include any necessary details.

Script:
- "Hi [Customer's Name]! This is a quick reminder from [Your Name at Dealership] about your appointment tomorrow at [Time] to see the [Vehicle Model]. We're looking forward to meeting you and will have everything ready for your visit. Please let me know if anything changes!"

Key Points:
- Keep the reminder clear, friendly, and short.
- Reassure them that the vehicle will be ready to encourage commitment.
- Offer an easy option for rescheduling if needed, showing flexibility.

3.4. Voicemail Script for No-Shows

Leaving a voicemail for a customer who didn't show up allows you to express understanding and invite them to reschedule. This approach is helpful when the customer may not be available for a direct conversation.

Script:
- "Hi [Customer's Name], this is [Your Name] from [Dealership]. I noticed we missed you at our appointment for the [Vehicle Model] earlier, and I just wanted to reach out in case there's anything I can do to help. I'd be happy to work with your schedule and find a better time. Feel free to call me back at [Your Phone Number] when you're ready. Looking forward to helping you soon!"

Key Points:
- Acknowledge the missed appointment politely without making them feel guilty.
- Offer to reschedule in a way that accommodates their schedule.
- Leave your contact information clearly, making it easy for them to follow up.

3.5. Email Follow-Up After a Rescheduled Appointment

If a customer reschedules, a follow-up email confirming the new date and time can reinforce their commitment and keep the appointment top-of-mind.

Email:
Subject Line: "Confirmation of Your Rescheduled Appointment"
Body: "Hello [Customer's Name],
Thank you for rescheduling! This is a quick confirmation of your upcoming appointment to see the [Vehicle Model] at [New Date and Time]. We're looking forward to welcoming you at [Dealership Location] and making sure everything is ready for your visit. If anything changes, please feel free to reach out at [Your Contact Info].
Best regards,
[Your Name, Dealership Name]"

Key Points:
- Confirm the new appointment details to reinforce their commitment.
- Keep the message professional, friendly, and easy to reference.
- Offer flexibility for changes, showing that you respect their time and schedule.

Conclusion: Crafting Follow-Up Messages that Drive Engagement

Effective follow-up calls and messages play a crucial role in appointment-setting success. By tailoring your follow-up approach to the specific situation—whether it's a missed appointment, an objection, or a reminder—you can keep customers engaged,

Chapter VII

overcome hesitations, and encourage them to take the next step in the car-buying journey. Use these scripts to maintain professionalism, empathy, and a customer-focused approach in every follow-up interaction.

Section 4. Dealing with Tough Objections During Follow-Ups

Objections are common in follow-up conversations, especially when customers are still weighing their options or have hesitations. Addressing tough objections effectively requires empathy, clear communication, and a solution-oriented approach. Rather than viewing objections as barriers, consider them as opportunities to understand the customer's needs better and provide tailored responses that encourage them to re-engage. Here are strategies and scripts for managing some of the most challenging objections during follow-ups.

4.1. "I'm Still Comparing Options"
Customers often hesitate if they're still considering other dealerships or vehicles. This objection can be challenging because they haven't ruled out the dealership, but they also aren't committed yet. The key is to acknowledge their decision-making process and highlight what makes your dealership or vehicle uniquely suited to their needs.

> **Script**:
> "I completely understand—you want to make the best choice! Many of our customers also compare options, and what they tell us is that after seeing the [Vehicle Model] and the level of service here, they felt confident in their choice. I'd be happy to go over any questions you might have to help with your decision."
>
> **Key Points**:
> - Acknowledge their need to explore options to validate their approach.
> - Subtly reinforce the benefits of your dealership and the vehicle without pressuring them.
> - Offer to assist with any questions, positioning yourself as a helpful resource.

4.2. "The Price Seems Too High"
Price objections are common and can feel challenging, especially if the customer is comparing your offer to competitors. It's important to reinforce the value of the vehicle and the dealership experience without seeming defensive or inflexible.

> **Script**:
> "I understand! We pride ourselves on competitive pricing, and this [Vehicle Model] is priced based on its excellent condition and the value it offers. Would it be helpful if I shared some of the reasons other customers have found this price to be a worthwhile investment? Or we can look at financing options to make it work within your budget."
>
> **Key Points**:

- Emphasize value rather than justifying the price outright.
- Offer to discuss financing to open up affordability options.
- Invite them to explore specific aspects of the vehicle that justify the price, like condition or unique features.

4.3. "I'm Not Ready to Make a Decision"

Sometimes, customers express reluctance because they're not fully prepared to commit. This may indicate they're looking for reassurance or need more information before moving forward. Acknowledging their timing while gently reminding them of the vehicle's popularity can encourage them to take the next step sooner.

Script:
"I completely understand, and the last thing we want is for you to feel rushed. Just to let you know, though, this [Vehicle Model] has been generating a lot of interest, and we don't want you to miss out if it's the right one for you. I'd be happy to answer any remaining questions or set up a time for you to come by and revisit it when you're ready."

Key Points:
- Respect their timing and need for a careful decision.
- Create a sense of urgency by mentioning the vehicle's popularity.
- Keep the invitation open-ended, offering help when they're ready.

4.4. "I've Found Another Vehicle Elsewhere"

When a customer mentions they've found a similar vehicle elsewhere, it can feel like a direct comparison. Rather than competing on price or features, focus on the quality of the experience you can offer and highlight the dealership's commitment to long-term customer satisfaction.

Script:
"That's great to hear! I'm glad you found another option you like. I'd like to mention that one of the things our customers value most is the peace of mind they get from working with [Dealership Name], knowing we're here to support them well beyond the purchase. Let me know if you'd like to explore options with us or discuss any of the services we offer for long-term care."

Key Points:
- Respect their decision without dismissing their interest in other options.
- Emphasize the dealership's reputation for customer care and long-term support.
- Keep the conversation open-ended, reminding them of your availability if they need anything.

4.5. "I'm Waiting for a Better Deal"

Chapter VII

Some customers hesitate because they're hoping for a future discount or promotion. To address this, acknowledge their budgeting concerns while reinforcing that the current pricing is competitive and in line with market value.

Script:
"I understand completely! Budgeting is so important, and I can assure you that we've priced this [Vehicle Model] very competitively to reflect its value. Waiting is always an option, of course, but because we're seeing strong interest in this model, I'd hate for you to miss out if it's a good fit. If there's anything specific holding you back, I'd be happy to discuss how we can make it work within your budget."

Key Points:
- Reinforce the fairness of the current pricing without sounding defensive.
- Highlight the vehicle's popularity to encourage a timely decision.
- Offer assistance in finding a solution, showing you're willing to work within their budget if possible.

4.6. "I Don't Have Time to Visit Right Now"

If a customer cites lack of time as a reason to delay, offer flexible options like a virtual tour or video call to keep them engaged. By accommodating their busy schedule, you increase the likelihood of rekindling their interest and securing a future visit.

Script:
"I completely understand! We all have busy schedules. If it helps, I'd be happy to set up a quick virtual tour so you can get a closer look at the [Vehicle Model] without needing to come in just yet. Whenever you're ready for an in-person visit, we'll be here to make it as easy as possible."

Key Points:
- Respect their schedule constraints, showing flexibility.
- Offer a low-commitment option (like a virtual tour) to keep them engaged.
- Maintain a service-oriented tone, reinforcing that you're available when they're ready.

4.7. "I Need to Talk to My Partner First"

When customers mention discussing with a partner, they're often in the final stages of decision-making. This is a natural part of the process, so respect their need for consultation and offer your assistance in answering any additional questions.

Script:
"Of course! Making a big purchase is definitely a decision worth discussing. I'd be happy to meet with both of you at a time that works for you or provide any information that might help your partner feel confident about the decision. Just let me know how I can assist!"

Key Points:
- Acknowledge the importance of consulting with a partner, showing empathy.
- Offer to meet with them both or answer additional questions to support their decision.
- Keep the tone respectful and supportive, reinforcing your willingness to help.

Conclusion: Handling Objections with Confidence and Empathy

When customers raise tough objections during follow-up conversations, it's an opportunity to demonstrate the dealership's commitment to understanding and meeting their needs. By responding professionally, empathizing with their concerns, and offering flexible solutions, you can turn hesitation into interest and bring them closer to a purchase decision. Each of these strategies is designed to address specific objections while keeping the customer relationship strong and focused on their best interests.

Chapter VIII

BUILDING LONG-TERM SKILLS AND SUCCESS

Section 1. Techniques for Maintaining Control Over the Conversation

Keeping control of the conversation is essential in follow-ups, especially when customers may be uncertain or raise objections. Maintaining control doesn't mean dominating the conversation; rather, it's about guiding it toward a productive outcome, ensuring that the dialogue remains positive and goal-focused. Here are strategies and techniques to help you stay in control while addressing customer needs effectively.

1.1. Start with a Clear Purpose for the Call
Beginning with a focused purpose sets the tone and gives direction to the conversation. When customers understand why you're calling, they're more likely to stay on track, making it easier for you to guide the discussion.

> **Script**:
> "Hi [Customer's Name], it's [Your Name] from [Dealership]. I'm following up on our previous conversation to see if there's anything more I can do to help with your interest in the [Vehicle Model]. Do you have a few minutes to chat?"
>
> **Key Points**:
> - State your purpose clearly to avoid wandering into unrelated topics.
> - Keep the introduction friendly but goal-oriented, so the customer understands the reason for the call.
> - Confirm their availability to show respect for their time and establish control early.

1.2. Ask Open-Ended Questions to Keep Engagement

Open-ended questions encourage the customer to share their thoughts, giving you insights to steer the conversation effectively. These questions allow you to understand their hesitations and keep the dialogue moving toward resolution.

> **Script**:
> "I'd love to hear more about what's most important to you in a vehicle. Could you share a bit about your main priorities?"

Key Points:
- Use open-ended questions to gather information without pressuring the customer.
- Listen actively to their responses, which will help you direct the conversation in a way that addresses their needs.
- Tailor follow-up questions based on their answers to maintain flow and engagement.

1.3. Acknowledge and Address Objections Concisely

When an objection arises, acknowledge it respectfully but keep your response concise. Addressing objections directly and confidently keeps the conversation from derailing and brings it back to the value of visiting the dealership.

Script:
"I understand, pricing is a big consideration. What I can tell you is that our current offers make the [Vehicle Model] a great value. If you'd like, I can go over some of the financing options that might work within your budget."

Key Points:
- Show empathy by acknowledging the objection first.
- Keep your response brief and relevant, addressing the concern without getting sidetracked.
- Transition smoothly to a potential solution, helping the customer see options instead of obstacles.

1.4. Guide the Conversation with "Soft Commands"

Soft commands are polite, suggestive statements that guide the customer without sounding forceful. They provide subtle direction and help you keep the conversation focused on moving toward a positive outcome.

Script:
"Let's go over some of the key features again, I think you'll see how well this model aligns with what you're looking for."

Key Points:
- Use phrases like "Let's go over..." or "Why don't we look at..." to gently guide the customer.
- Soft commands maintain control without creating resistance, as they are framed as helpful suggestions.
- Focus on statements that reinforce the value of the vehicle or the appointment, subtly steering the customer back to the key points.

1.5. Use Transitional Statements to Avoid Interruptions

If the customer begins to veer off-topic or express hesitations that could derail the conversation, use transitional statements to bring the focus back. Transitional statements acknowledge the customer's point while smoothly redirecting them.

Chapter VIII

Script:
"That's a good point. And speaking of what you mentioned, one of the reasons our customers love this [Vehicle Model] is the way it delivers on those specific needs."

Key Points:
- Acknowledge the customer's comment to show you're listening.
- Use transitions to guide the conversation back to the main purpose.
- Keep the tone positive and supportive, making the shift feel natural rather than forced.

1.6. Avoid Open-Ended Departures and Keep Next Steps Clear

Avoid ending the conversation with vague statements like "Let us know if you need anything." Instead, establish a clear next step, whether it's scheduling a follow-up call, booking an appointment, or sending additional information. This ensures the conversation has a defined outcome.

Script:
"Great! I'll go ahead and set up a time for you to come by and see the vehicle in person. Does [Day and Time] work for you, or would you prefer [Alternative Time]?"

Key Points:
- Avoid open-ended conclusions that leave the next steps unclear.
- Suggest specific actions that encourage them to move forward in the process.
- By confirming the next steps, you maintain control and keep the momentum of the conversation.

1.7. Use Recap Statements to Reinforce Key Points
Throughout the conversation, summarize key points to ensure the customer remains focused on what's most important. Recap statements help reinforce value, address concerns, and keep the dialogue cohesive.

Script:
"Just to recap, you mentioned that safety and affordability are priorities, and the [Vehicle Model] really stands out with its safety ratings and competitive pricing. Let's go over a few options that could work for you."

Key Points:
- Recap statements ensure both you and the customer are aligned on key points.
- Use recaps to reinforce benefits and demonstrate that you're listening to their needs.
- Recaps serve as natural points to steer the conversation back to value-focused topics.

Chapter VIII

Conclusion: Guiding the Conversation with Confidence and Respect
Maintaining control of follow-up conversations is about creating a focused and productive dialogue. By using techniques like open-ended questions, soft commands, and recap statements, you can guide customers toward a positive outcome without sounding forceful. Keeping the conversation on track while showing empathy and understanding not only helps resolve objections but also builds trust and reinforces your commitment to their needs.

Section 2. Best Practices for Building Rapport and Trust

Building rapport and trust with customers is essential for creating positive and lasting connections. When customers feel comfortable and valued, they're more likely to engage openly, share their true needs, and trust you as a partner in their car-buying journey. Here are best practices for establishing rapport and trust, especially during follow-up conversations, that strengthen relationships and increase the likelihood of successful outcomes.

2.1. Start with a Warm, Personalized Greeting

A friendly, personalized greeting sets a positive tone for the conversation and shows the customer that you remember and value them. Small details, like using their name or referencing previous interactions, can go a long way in making the conversation feel genuine.

Script:
"Hi [Customer's Name], it's great to connect again! How have you been since we last spoke about the [Vehicle Model]?"

Key Points:
- Use the customer's name to make the greeting personal and engaging.
- Reference previous conversations or details about their needs to show you're invested in their experience.
- Keep the greeting warm and friendly, setting a positive tone from the start.

2.2. Listen Actively and Show Empathy
Active listening is one of the most powerful ways to build trust. By truly listening to the customer and responding with empathy, you demonstrate that you value their concerns and are committed to understanding their needs.

Script:
"I understand that finding the right vehicle can be a big decision. It sounds like [specific concern] is really important to you. Let's see how we can address that together."

Key Points:
- Acknowledge their feelings and concerns to show empathy.
- Paraphrase their statements to confirm your understanding.

- Let them feel heard before offering solutions, building trust and credibility.

2.3. Share Relevant Personal Experiences or Stories

When appropriate, sharing a relatable story or experience can help humanize the interaction and make you seem approachable. This can be especially effective if the story aligns with the customer's needs or concerns, as it shows you genuinely understand what they're going through.

- **Script**:
- "I completely get where you're coming from. I remember helping a customer last month who also wanted a car with [feature], and they found the [Vehicle Model] was a perfect fit. I think you'll feel the same!"

- **Key Points**:
- Keep the story brief and relevant to the customer's interests.
- Share experiences that show empathy and understanding, not just for the sake of storytelling.
- Be genuine to avoid sounding rehearsed or insincere.

2.4. Use Positive Language to Reinforce Solutions

Positive language helps keep the conversation constructive and solution-focused, showing customers that you're committed to making their experience pleasant. This helps alleviate concerns and reinforces the dealership as a welcoming and supportive place.

Script:
"Great question! One thing I think you'll love about the [Vehicle Model] is how well it meets [specific need]. I'm confident we can make this a fantastic choice for you."

Key Points:
- Focus on positive language, such as "great," "fantastic," and "confident."
- Reassure them that you're focused on meeting their needs, making them feel supported.
- Avoid overly technical or complex language, as it may create unnecessary distance.

2.5. Be Transparent and Honest

Customers appreciate honesty, especially when it comes to discussing options or addressing potential limitations. If a feature or financing option they want isn't available, be upfront while framing the conversation around finding the best possible alternative.

Script:

"I want to be completely transparent with you. While this model may not have [specific feature], it does offer [alternative feature] that many of our customers find equally valuable. Let's take a closer look together to see if it aligns with what you're looking for."

Key Points:
- Approach limitations or unavailable features with honesty and empathy.
- Focus on alternatives or other benefits, showing you're committed to finding a solution.
- Maintain a supportive tone to avoid any defensiveness or negativity.

2.6. Follow Up Promptly with Promised Information

If you commit to sending additional information or resources, follow up promptly. Doing so demonstrates reliability and respect for the customer's time, both of which contribute to building trust and showing that you keep your word.

Script:
"Hi [Customer's Name], as promised, I'm sending over the information on [requested feature or financing option]. Let me know if there's anything else you'd like to know. I'm here to help however I can!"

Key Points:
- Follow through with promised actions, like sending information or providing updates, as soon as possible.
- Reaffirm your commitment to being a dependable resource.
- Use follow-ups to re-engage and show you value their time and interest.

2.7. Express Genuine Appreciation for Their Interest

Showing gratitude goes a long way in making customers feel valued. Whether they're in the early stages of consideration or have visited multiple times, expressing appreciation reinforces the dealership's commitment to positive customer relationships.

Script:
"Thank you so much for considering us in your search, [Customer's Name]. We know there are a lot of choices out there, and we're here to make this experience as easy and enjoyable as possible."

Key Points:
- Use language that conveys sincere appreciation and gratitude.
- Let them know their business is important to you and the dealership.
- Make them feel acknowledged for their consideration, even if they haven't yet made a commitment.

2.8. Encourage Open Communication

Chapter VIII

Building trust involves making it clear that the customer can openly share any questions, concerns, or hesitations with you. By inviting open communication, you establish a safe space for them to discuss their needs, making it easier for you to address any hidden objections or issues.

Script:
"Please don't hesitate to share any questions or thoughts you have. I'm here to help in any way I can and make sure you feel completely comfortable with your choice."

Key Points:
- Encourage them to be open, creating a transparent and trusting environment.
- Reassure them that all questions are welcome, reinforcing your dedication to helping.
- Make it clear that your role is to support them, not just to make a sale.

Conclusion: Building a Foundation of Trust for Long-Term Relationships

Building rapport and trust during follow-up conversations requires empathy, transparency, and a genuine commitment to customer satisfaction. By using these best practices, you can create a positive and supportive environment where customers feel valued and understood. This foundation of trust not only increases the likelihood of immediate sales but also fosters long-term relationships that benefit both the customer and the dealership.

Chapter IX

MEASURING PERFORMANCE AND CONTINUOUS IMPROVEMENT

Section 1. Key Metrics for Tracking Appointment Success (Show Rates, Conversions)

Tracking appointment success through key metrics is essential for understanding what works, identifying areas for improvement, and refining the appointment-setting process. Show rates, conversion rates, and other related metrics offer valuable insights that can drive continuous improvement for both Business Development Center (BDC) and Internet Sales departments. Here, we'll cover the most important metrics to monitor, why they matter, and how to use them to optimize performance.

1.1. Show Rate

The show rate is one of the most critical metrics for measuring the effectiveness of appointment-setting efforts. It represents the percentage of scheduled appointments that result in customers physically showing up at the dealership. A high show rate indicates that the appointment-setting process is successfully motivating customers to follow through, while a low show rate suggests potential issues in scheduling, confirmation, or customer engagement.

- **Formula**:
  - **Show Rate (%)** = (Number of Appointments Shown / Number of Appointments Set) × 100

- **Key Insights**:
  - A high show rate reflects effective communication, quality customer engagement, and well-managed appointment confirmations.
  - A low show rate may indicate the need for improved follow-up strategies, more effective reminder systems, or adjustments to appointment-setting scripts to increase urgency.

- **Target Benchmark**:
  - Aim for a show rate of at least 50–60%. Depending on the dealership and market, top-performing BDC teams often exceed 70%.

1.2. Appointment-to-Sales Conversion Rate

The appointment-to-sales conversion rate measures the effectiveness of appointments in generating actual sales. This metric goes beyond simply getting customers through the door—it evaluates whether those who show up are being converted into buyers. A high conversion rate indicates that the team is setting quality appointments with motivated customers and that the dealership is effective in the in-person sales process.

Formula:
- **Appointment-to-Sales Conversion Rate (%)** = (Number of Sales from Appointments / Number of Appointments Shown) × 100

Key Insights:
- A high conversion rate demonstrates that appointments are attracting serious buyers, and it reflects well on the in-person sales team's closing ability.
- A low conversion rate suggests a need to reassess the types of leads being pursued, the quality of appointment setting, or even sales team training on converting in-store visits.

Target Benchmark:
- Most dealerships should aim for a conversion rate of around 50–60%. Strong conversion rates can be as high as 70% in high-performing sales environments.

1.3. Appointment Set Rate

The appointment set rate measures the percentage of total leads that result in a scheduled appointment. This metric is a strong indicator of how effectively the BDC or Internet Sales team is turning inquiries and interest into solid appointments. A high appointment set rate indicates efficient outreach efforts, good initial customer engagement, and skillful handling of inbound leads.

Formula:
- **Appointment Set Rate (%)** = (Number of Appointments Set / Total Number of Leads) × 100

Key Insights:
- A high appointment set rate suggests the team is skilled at engaging leads and encouraging them to commit to a dealership visit.
- A low appointment set rate may indicate ineffective initial outreach or a need to improve response times, scripting, or lead engagement strategies.

Target Benchmark:
- Typically, aim for an appointment set rate of at least 40–50% for inbound leads and 25–30% for outbound leads, as outbound prospects may require more effort to convert into appointments.

1.4. Lead-to-Sale Conversion Rate

The lead-to-sale conversion rate measures the percentage of total leads that ultimately result in a sale. This metric provides a holistic view of the entire lead-to-sale process, from initial engagement to final purchase, and helps determine the overall effectiveness of the team's appointment-setting and follow-up efforts.

Formula:
- **Lead-to-Sale Conversion Rate (%)** = (Number of Sales / Total Number of Leads) × 100

Key Insights:
- A high lead-to-sale conversion rate indicates a strong, effective sales funnel where leads are successfully nurtured from initial interest to purchase.
- A low conversion rate may suggest issues in various parts of the funnel, including lead qualification, appointment-setting quality, follow-up processes, or closing techniques.

Target Benchmark:
- Lead-to-sale conversion rates vary by industry, but in automotive sales, aim for 10–20%. Higher rates suggest a particularly efficient lead management and appointment-setting process.

1.5. Show Rate by Source

Understanding the show rate by lead source (e.g., inbound calls, online inquiries, third-party leads) helps identify which sources are most effective in delivering engaged customers. This insight allows the dealership to focus resources on the highest-performing channels and refine strategies for lower-performing ones.

Formula:
- Calculate the show rate separately for each source, following the same formula as the overall show rate.

Key Insights:
- Lead sources with high show rates indicate channels that are delivering motivated, ready-to-buy customers.
- Sources with low show rates may need adjusted messaging, different follow-up techniques, or re-evaluation of the quality of leads they generate.

Target Benchmark:
- Aim to maintain consistently high show rates across key sources, with an ideal range of 50–60% or higher for most sources.

1.6. Customer Feedback Score on Appointment Experience

While not a direct metric, customer feedback provides qualitative insight into the effectiveness of appointment-setting and the customer experience. Positive feedback reflects strong customer engagement and satisfaction, while negative feedback may point to areas for improvement in communication, convenience, or sales approach.

How to Measure:
- Conduct post-appointment surveys asking customers about their experience, ease of scheduling, and whether they felt their expectations were met.

Key Insights:
- Positive feedback validates that the current appointment-setting process is customer-centric and effective.
- Negative feedback highlights specific areas for improvement, such as streamlining the scheduling process, better communication, or more accurate vehicle information.

Target Benchmark:
- Aim for high satisfaction scores (4.5 out of 5 or above) on appointment experience surveys.

Conclusion: Using Key Metrics to Drive Improvement

Tracking these key metrics provides a clear picture of the effectiveness of your appointment-setting strategies and helps identify specific areas for improvement. Regularly monitoring show rates, conversion rates, and appointment set rates enables the team to make data-driven adjustments, refine follow-up techniques, and enhance customer engagement. By consistently aiming to improve these metrics, the dealership can build a more efficient, customer-focused appointment-setting process that drives sales and fosters lasting relationships.

Section 2. Self-Assessment Techniques

Continuous improvement in appointment setting and sales requires regular self-assessment. Self-assessment enables sales and BDC team members to identify strengths, recognize areas for growth, and refine techniques to drive higher performance. Here are proven self-assessment techniques that can enhance individual skills, build confidence, and keep the team aligned with dealership goals.

2.1. Review Call Recordings and Emails

Listening to call recordings or reviewing email exchanges allows team members to reflect on their interactions with customers. This process provides valuable insights into tone, responsiveness, and effectiveness, highlighting areas for improvement and reinforcing successful strategies.

How to Implement:
- Regularly set aside time to review recordings of your own calls and emails.
- Pay attention to the clarity of your messaging, tone of voice, and customer reactions.

- Look for any patterns in the conversations that result in either successful or missed appointments.

Key Focus Areas:
- **Tone and Energy**: Assess if your tone was friendly, professional, and engaging.
- **Clarity and Conciseness**: Identify any parts of the conversation that could be clearer or more direct.
- **Response to Objections**: Evaluate how well you handled objections and whether your responses were effective.

2.2. Set Personal Performance Benchmarks and Track Progress

Setting personal benchmarks for key metrics, such as show rate or appointment-to-sale conversion rate, allows you to gauge your progress over time. Tracking your results helps to visualize improvement and stay motivated by identifying how close you are to achieving your goals.

How to Implement:
- Choose 1-2 metrics to focus on each month, such as increasing your appointment set rate by 10%.
- Track these metrics weekly and review them at the end of the month.
- Adjust your approach based on your performance relative to these benchmarks.

Key Focus Areas:
- **Show Rate Improvement**: Set a realistic target increase for the percentage of appointments that result in showroom visits.
- **Conversion Efficiency**: Track your ability to move from setting an appointment to closing a sale.

2.3. Use Role-Playing for Skill Refinement

Role-playing scenarios with a peer or manager can improve specific skills, such as handling objections or creating urgency. This allows team members to practice techniques in a safe environment, receive immediate feedback, and make adjustments before applying them with actual customers.

- **How to Implement:**
- Practice common scenarios like responding to price objections, handling reschedule requests, or confirming appointments.
- Rotate roles, with one person acting as the customer to provide realistic feedback.
- After each role-play, discuss what worked well and where improvements could be made.

- **Key Focus Areas:**

- **Objection Handling**: Practice responses to common objections and assess the effectiveness of your replies.
- **Building Urgency**: Test out language that creates urgency without sounding pushy.
- **Maintaining Control**: Practice techniques that keep the conversation focused and moving toward a successful outcome.

2.4. Reflect After Each Customer Interaction

A quick post-interaction reflection allows you to immediately assess what went well and what could be improved. This habit of reflecting on each call or email keeps your skills sharp and builds self-awareness.

How to Implement:
- After each call or email interaction, take a moment to ask yourself:
    "What did I do well in this conversation?"
    "What could I have done differently to improve the outcome?"
- Write down brief notes on key insights to identify patterns over time.

Key Focus Areas:
- **Successes**: Identify aspects of the interaction that led to positive responses from the customer.
- **Growth Opportunities**: Recognize any moments where you felt the conversation could have gone better.
- **Follow-Up Strategy**: Reflect on the next steps and what can be done to maintain the customer's interest.

2.5. Request Feedback from Peers or Supervisors

Sometimes, an outside perspective can reveal insights you might miss on your own. Asking for feedback from trusted colleagues or supervisors gives you constructive input that can strengthen your skills and performance.

How to Implement:
- Ask a peer or supervisor to review specific call recordings or email exchanges.
- Request specific feedback on areas where you'd like to improve, such as objection handling or building rapport.
- Be open to constructive criticism, and take notes on feedback to apply in future interactions.

Key Focus Areas:
- **Customer Engagement**: Assess if your approach is engaging and supportive.
- **Efficiency**: Get feedback on whether your responses are clear, concise, and effective.

- **Areas for Growth**: Identify any blind spots or areas for improvement that you may not have noticed.

2.6. Evaluate Appointment Outcomes Weekly

Tracking the outcome of each appointment, whether successful or not, helps you understand which techniques work best and which may need refining. By reviewing outcomes on a weekly basis, you can make data-informed adjustments that enhance future performance.

How to Implement:
- Record the result of each appointment (show, no-show, or reschedule) and any insights gained from the interaction.
- At the end of each week, review your outcomes to spot trends in successful appointments versus no-shows or missed sales.
- Use these insights to adjust your approach to setting, confirming, or following up on appointments.

Key Focus Areas:
- **Success Rate**: Monitor which follow-up techniques yield higher show and conversion rates.
- **Common Challenges**: Identify recurring obstacles, such as objections or scheduling conflicts, to refine your approach.
- **Process Adjustments**: Use the insights to improve areas like confirmation timing, reminder methods, or closing techniques.

2.7. Set and Review Monthly Improvement Goals

At the start of each month, set specific improvement goals to build on your skills and track how these goals impact your performance. Goals provide direction and help you measure incremental progress, building both competence and confidence over time.

How to Implement:
- Identify 1-3 specific goals related to your appointment-setting performance, such as improving show rates or handling objections more effectively.
- Track progress weekly, and review your results at the end of the month to evaluate growth.
- Reflect on what worked well and plan new goals based on areas that need further improvement.

Key Focus Areas:
- **Performance Metrics**: Choose goals aligned with key metrics, like increasing conversion rates or reducing no-shows.
- **Skill Development**: Set goals around specific skills, such as mastering new scripts or building rapport.
- **Consistency**: Aim for consistent improvement in performance areas, reinforcing habits that lead to success.

Chapter IX

Conclusion: Building Long-Term Skills Through Self-Assessment

Self-assessment is a powerful tool for continuous improvement in appointment-setting and sales. By regularly reviewing calls, setting benchmarks, engaging in role-play, and seeking feedback, you gain a deeper understanding of your strengths and areas for growth. Consistently applying these techniques helps you develop confidence, improve customer engagement, and maximize your success rates. Ultimately, self-assessment fosters a proactive approach to personal and professional development that supports long-term success in the dealership environment.

Section 3. Tips for Continuous Improvement and Professional Growth

In the fast-paced dealership environment, striving for continuous improvement is essential for success. By actively pursuing professional growth, you can stay adaptable, refine your skills, and keep up with industry best practices. This section provides actionable tips to foster continuous improvement and professional growth, enabling you to advance your career and enhance your effectiveness in setting appointments and closing sales.

3.1. Stay Updated on Industry Trends and Best Practices

The automotive industry and customer expectations are constantly evolving. Staying informed about new trends, tools, and techniques in car sales and customer engagement can give you a competitive edge and inspire fresh approaches to appointment setting and sales.

How to Implement:
- Follow reputable industry sources, such as automotive news websites, dealership publications, and training platforms.
- Join online communities or forums where sales professionals share insights and experiences.
- Set aside time each week to review new information, articles, or case studies relevant to dealership sales.

Key Focus Areas:
- **Customer Expectations**: Keep up with what customers are looking for in their car-buying journey.
- **Sales Techniques**: Learn about new or updated sales techniques to enhance appointment-setting success.
- **Technology**: Explore emerging CRM tools and software that can streamline appointment setting and customer follow-ups.

3.2. Participate in Ongoing Training and Development

Formal training helps deepen your skills and exposes you to new strategies for handling customer interactions, objections, and follow-ups. Regular training reinforces key concepts and builds confidence.

How to Implement:
- Attend dealership-sponsored training sessions, webinars, or workshops.
- Seek out online courses or certifications focused on sales techniques, customer service, or automotive industry knowledge.
- Set professional development goals for each quarter to focus on specific skills you want to strengthen.

Key Focus Areas:
- **Sales Fundamentals**: Reinforce basics like rapport-building, needs analysis, and objection handling.
- **Specialized Skills**: Target specific skills, such as digital customer engagement, phone etiquette, or cross-selling.
- **Product Knowledge**: Enhance your knowledge of the vehicles you're selling to increase credibility and customer trust.

3.3. Seek Mentorship and Build a Support Network

Learning from seasoned professionals can accelerate your growth and provide you with valuable insights. Mentorship and networking expose you to different perspectives and provide support in navigating challenges.

How to Implement:
- Reach out to a more experienced colleague or manager and ask if they'd be open to regular mentorship meetings.
- Join local or online industry groups to connect with other sales professionals.
- Attend dealership or industry events to build a network of peers and mentors.

Key Focus Areas:
- **Experience Sharing**: Gain insights from others' experiences, including successful tactics and lessons learned.
- **Feedback and Advice**: Seek constructive feedback on specific areas, like appointment-setting strategies or customer interactions.
- **Long-Term Growth**: Use your support network to discuss career goals and get advice on progression within the dealership.

3.4. Set Personal Performance Goals and Track Progress Regularly

Personal goals provide direction and motivation, helping you stay focused on continuous improvement. By setting measurable goals and tracking your progress, you can see tangible results and stay accountable to your growth objectives.

How to Implement:
- Set monthly and quarterly goals based on performance metrics like show rates, conversions, or customer satisfaction scores.
- Use a tracking tool, spreadsheet, or CRM to monitor your results over time.

- Reflect on your progress at the end of each month, adjusting your goals as needed.

Key Focus Areas:
- **Incremental Improvements**: Focus on small, achievable targets that build over time.
- **Skill Mastery**: Set goals for specific skills, such as improving follow-up techniques or increasing show rates.
- **Accountability**: Review your progress regularly to stay motivated and adapt your strategies as needed.

3.5. Embrace Feedback as a Tool for Growth

Feedback, whether from supervisors, colleagues, or customers, is a valuable resource for improvement. Constructive feedback highlights areas you might not notice on your own, providing opportunities to refine your approach.

How to Implement:
- Ask for feedback after key interactions, such as follow-up calls, sales meetings, or customer appointments.
- Be open to feedback from all sources, and approach it with a growth mindset.
- Use feedback as actionable input, implementing suggested changes and monitoring the results.

Key Focus Areas:
- **Self-Reflection**: Reflect on feedback honestly, focusing on both strengths and areas for growth.
- **Actionable Steps**: Turn feedback into specific actions you can implement immediately.
- **Continuous Improvement**: Regularly seek feedback to ensure you're on the right track and making progress.

3.6. Engage in Self-Evaluation and Reflection
Self-assessment allows you to objectively evaluate your strengths, weaknesses, and overall performance. By reflecting on your actions and outcomes, you gain clarity on what's working well and what needs adjustment.

How to Implement:
- After each appointment or call, take a few moments to consider what went well and what could have been improved.
- Maintain a journal or notes to track insights gained from your reflections.
- Use your self-assessment insights to guide your focus areas for future interactions.

Key Focus Areas:

- **Self-Awareness**: Recognize your unique strengths and areas where you need more development.
- **Pattern Recognition**: Look for recurring patterns, such as challenges in specific customer interactions or objections.
- **Improvement Plan**: Use your reflections to set targeted improvement goals and practice new techniques.

7. Stay Organized and Use Time Management Strategies

Organizational skills and effective time management help you stay productive, reduce stress, and make the most of each customer interaction. A well-organized schedule enables you to prioritize tasks like follow-ups, appointment confirmations, and customer outreach.

How to Implement:
- Use a scheduling tool or CRM to organize appointments, set reminders, and track follow-ups.
- Prioritize daily tasks and focus on high-impact activities first, such as reaching out to warm leads.
- Allocate time each day for key activities like lead follow-up, training, or goal-setting.

Key Focus Areas:
- **Efficiency**: Streamline your processes to ensure you're making the best use of your time.
- **Prioritization**: Identify which tasks drive the most results and prioritize them.
- **Consistency**: Build a structured daily routine that supports your performance and growth.

3.8. Celebrate Wins and Learn from Challenges

Acknowledging your achievements and learning from setbacks boosts motivation and resilience. By celebrating wins, you reinforce positive behaviors; while analyzing challenges helps you find solutions for future success.

How to Implement:
- Recognize both big and small achievements, whether it's closing a difficult sale or improving your show rate.
- After setbacks, identify what went wrong and brainstorm ways to handle similar situations better in the future.
- Share your wins and lessons learned with peers or mentors to build a support network.

Key Focus Areas:
- **Positive Reinforcement**: Celebrate wins to build confidence and motivation.

Chapter IX

- **Growth Mindset**: View challenges as opportunities for learning and improvement.
- **Support System**: Share your experiences to foster a positive, growth-oriented team culture.

Conclusion: Fostering a Mindset of Growth and Excellence

Continuous improvement and professional growth require dedication, adaptability, and a proactive mindset. By staying updated, setting goals, seeking feedback, and engaging in self-assessment, you can continually refine your skills and drive success in dealership appointment setting and sales. Embracing a growth-oriented approach not only boosts your performance but also positions you as an asset to the dealership and paves the way for long-term career advancement.

Chapter X

Utilizing Technology in the Appointment Process

Section 1. Tools for Tracking Leads and Scheduling Appointments

In a dealership environment, tracking leads and efficiently scheduling appointments is essential for converting interest into actual showroom visits and, ultimately, sales. Using a CRM tailored to the unique demands of auto dealerships is the cornerstone of effective lead management. In this section, we'll explore the tools and features within dealership-specific CRMs that facilitate seamless lead tracking, organized appointment scheduling, and structured follow-up processes to maximize show rates and optimize customer engagement.

1.1. Auto Dealership-Specific CRM Features

Auto dealership CRMs—like VinSolutions, ELEAD1ONE, and DealerSocket—are equipped with features that go beyond the traditional CRM functionalities to meet the specific needs of the automotive industry. These tools support a structured approach to tracking leads, managing appointments, and optimizing each customer interaction.

Comprehensive Lead Management
Auto dealership CRMs are designed to capture and track leads from multiple sources, such as website inquiries, inbound calls, social media, and walk-ins. This ensures a consistent flow of lead data that is accessible to the sales and BDC teams.
- **Multi-Channel Lead Capture**: Automatically imports leads from various channels, reducing the need for manual data entry.
- **Lead Scoring and Prioritization**: Enables teams to categorize leads based on potential interest, helping sales representatives focus on high-priority leads.

Appointment Scheduling and Alerts
Scheduling tools within the CRM allow the sales or BDC team to set up appointments quickly, helping to reduce no-show rates and ensure customers are committed to their time slots.

Chapter X

- **Appointment Calendar**: An integrated calendar displays available times, allowing teams to offer real-time scheduling options to customers.
- **Automatic Alerts**: CRM alerts notify sales reps and managers of upcoming appointments, follow-ups, or any other scheduled activities.

Customer Profiles and History Tracking

With dealership CRMs, customer profiles aggregate all past interactions, inquiries, purchases, and service appointments, providing a 360-degree view of each customer's journey.

- **Centralized Customer History**: View the entire customer journey within one profile, making follow-ups more personalized and relevant.
- **In-Depth Insights**: CRM profiles often display customer preferences, specific vehicle interests, and past interactions, allowing sales teams to engage customers more effectively.

1.2. Real-Time Data Access for Informed Engagement

Real-time access to data allows sales and BDC teams to provide accurate information on inventory, pricing, and promotions during appointments, creating a seamless experience for the customer. Auto dealership CRMs sync with inventory and pricing databases, enabling reps to make quick, data-driven decisions.

Inventory Integration

Real-time inventory integration helps sales teams know exactly what's available on the lot, reducing the risk of booking appointments for unavailable vehicles.

- **Vehicle Availability**: Sales reps can check in-stock vehicles instantly, ensuring they recommend only available options.
- **Pricing and Promotions**: Stay updated on current promotions or limited-time pricing, allowing reps to offer customers the latest deals.

Automated Data Updates

CRMs automatically update customer and inventory data, reflecting real-time changes across all touchpoints.

- **Lead Status Changes**: As leads progress through stages (e.g., initial inquiry to scheduled appointment), the CRM updates in real-time, keeping everyone on the same page.
- **Customer Notes and Preferences**: Updates on customer preferences and responses are stored centrally, allowing any team member to step in and offer a seamless experience.

1.3. CRM Tools to Support Appointment Cadences

Automated cadences ensure follow-up touchpoints are consistent and timely, maximizing the likelihood of successful engagements and minimizing lead attrition. Here's how dealership CRMs support these structured cadences:

Automated Appointment Reminders

A well-configured CRM sends reminders to customers at key intervals, such as 24 hours before the appointment and again on the day of.

- **Email and SMS Reminders**: Schedule automatic emails and texts to remind customers of their appointment, reducing no-shows and last-minute cancellations.
- **Personalized Reminder Templates**: Customize reminders with the customer's name, appointment details, and dealership contact information to reinforce a personalized touch.

Follow-Up Cadence Automation

CRMs allow dealerships to establish structured cadences based on lead behavior, ensuring timely follow-ups even if the lead doesn't convert on the first interaction.

- **Missed Appointment Cadence**: Automates a follow-up process if a customer misses their appointment, prompting rescheduling with a light, friendly approach.
- **Cold Lead Cadence**: Engages leads who haven't responded in a while, keeping the dealership top-of-mind with periodic touchpoints.

Customizable Cadence Settings for Different Lead Types

By categorizing leads (e.g., high-interest, warm, or cold), CRMs allow for differentiated follow-up strategies that align with each lead's engagement level.

- **High-Interest Leads**: More frequent touchpoints to encourage quick conversion.
- **General Interest Leads**: Moderate cadence to keep the lead warm without over-communicating.
- **Cold Leads**: Less frequent touchpoints to re-engage the customer over time.

1.4. Integrating Scheduling and Lead Tracking with BDC Operations

A well-integrated CRM system connects with Business Development Center (BDC) operations to enhance efficiency and streamline the customer journey from initial inquiry to appointment arrival.

Lead Distribution and Assignment

CRMs help streamline lead assignment based on criteria like lead type, salesperson availability, or customer preference, ensuring leads are handled by the best-suited representative.

- **Round-Robin Assignment**: Automates lead distribution to ensure a balanced workload across the BDC team.
- **Customized Assignment Rules**: Assign leads based on specific criteria, like language preference or geographic location, to increase conversion rates.

BDC Appointment Management Dashboard

Many dealership CRMs offer dashboards specifically for the BDC team, giving them a real-time overview of appointments, lead status, and pending follow-ups.

- **Daily Appointment View**: Shows all scheduled appointments for the day, allowing BDC reps to prepare for follow-ups and confirmations.
- **Lead Conversion Metrics**: Displays key metrics like show rates and conversion rates, helping BDC managers adjust strategies as needed.

Team Communication Features
Integrated messaging or tagging features within the CRM allow BDC and sales teams to coordinate seamlessly on lead status, appointment confirmations, and specific customer notes.

- **Internal Messaging**: BDC reps can notify sales reps when an appointment is confirmed or if there's an update on a specific lead.
- **Tagging and Notifications**: Tag specific team members in lead notes, alerting them to important updates or action items.

1.5. Leveraging Analytics and Reporting for Continuous Improvement
Advanced analytics and reporting features within CRMs help dealerships measure the effectiveness of their lead management and appointment-setting processes. Data-driven insights allow for continuous refinement of strategies to enhance conversion rates and customer satisfaction.

Show Rate Analysis
Track the percentage of leads that result in dealership visits, providing insight into appointment-setting effectiveness.

- **Daily and Monthly Show Rate Reports**: Evaluate show rates on a regular basis to spot patterns or identify peak times.
- **Appointment Source Comparison**: Compare show rates based on lead source (e.g., website inquiries vs. phone leads) to optimize marketing spend.

Conversion Rate Tracking
Monitor how many leads convert into sales after appointments, helping assess the overall efficiency of the appointment and sales process.

- **Lead-to-Sale Conversion Metrics**: Measure the end-to-end conversion journey from lead to sale, identifying stages where drop-off occurs.
- **Sales Team Performance Analysis**: Compare conversion rates across sales reps to identify high performers or potential areas for training.

Lead Aging and Follow-Up Success Rates
Track how long leads remain in the CRM before action is taken and measure the success rate of different follow-up cadences.

- **Lead Aging Reports**: Identify how quickly leads are being addressed to minimize aging leads that are less likely to convert.
- **Follow-Up Cadence Effectiveness**: Review the effectiveness of different follow-up frequencies and messaging to refine cadence strategies.

Conclusion: Enhancing Lead Tracking and Appointment Scheduling with CRMs

The tools provided by dealership CRMs offer comprehensive support for managing leads, scheduling appointments, and establishing effective cadences. By leveraging these CRM capabilities, dealerships can streamline the appointment-setting process, enhance communication with customers, and improve conversion rates. Well-integrated CRMs also enable cross-departmental collaboration, ensuring that the BDC, sales team, and management are aligned in tracking and engaging leads

Chapter X

effectively. The insights gathered through CRM analytics allow for continuous optimization, helping dealerships stay competitive and responsive to customer needs.

Section 2. Integrating CRM and Communication Platforms for Follow-Ups

Effective follow-up and consistent communication are essential for converting leads into in-store appointments and ultimately closing sales. In car dealerships, integrating Customer Relationship Management (CRM) systems with robust communication platforms enables teams to engage leads seamlessly through email, text, and phone, ensuring every lead receives timely and personalized attention. While CRMs excel in managing lead follow-ups and tracking interactions, they often don't address the unique in-store processes required to close a sale. This is where **SalesLeader**, a Dealer Sales Management system, plays a complementary role by optimizing in-dealership sales interactions and maximizing appointment conversion rates. SalesLeader does not integrate with CRMs, but it enhances their value by focusing on structured in-store processes once a customer arrives at the dealership.

2.1. Multi-Channel Communication Tools in Dealership CRMs

Auto dealership CRMs, such as VinSolutions, ELEAD1ONE, and DealerSocket, come with integrated communication tools that allow teams to manage customer interactions from a centralized platform, ensuring consistent and coordinated follow-ups.

Email Integration
Dealership CRMs allow for personalized and automated email communication, making it easy to set up appointment confirmations, reminders, and post-appointment thank-you messages.
- **Automated Follow-Up Emails**: CRMs enable automated email sequences to keep leads engaged over time.
- **Personalization**: Emails can be customized based on the customer's vehicle preferences, past interactions, and scheduled appointment details.

SMS and Text Messaging
Integrated SMS tools within CRMs allow teams to communicate with customers instantly via text. This is particularly effective for sending reminders, confirmations, and quick updates, as SMS open rates tend to be higher than email.
- **Quick Confirmations and Updates**: CRMs allow for real-time confirmation texts, keeping communication fast and efficient.
- **Scheduled SMS Reminders**: Automated text reminders ensure customers remember their appointments, which helps reduce no-show rates.

Call Tracking and Recording
Call management features allow CRMs to track and record phone interactions, which is helpful for quality control and performance tracking.

Chapter X

- **Call Tracking**: Ensures that every phone interaction is logged, giving teams a complete communication history.
- **Call Recording for Training**: Recordings enable managers to provide targeted feedback to improve phone interaction quality.

2.2. Automating Follow-Ups and Reminders with CRM Systems

Automation within CRMs plays a crucial role in ensuring that follow-ups are timely and consistent, without requiring constant manual effort. Automated follow-ups allow dealerships to nurture leads through a series of touchpoints that keep the dealership top-of-mind.

Structured Cadence Automation
Setting up a structured cadence within the CRM allows for consistent follow-ups based on lead activity and engagement level.
- **Appointment Reminder Cadences**: CRMs can send reminders to customers at key intervals, such as 24 hours before and one hour before the appointment.
- **Missed Appointment Follow-Ups**: Automate reminders if a customer misses an appointment, making it easy to offer rescheduling options.
- **Lead Nurturing Cadences**: For leads not yet ready to schedule, CRM automation can provide periodic updates on inventory, promotions, and relevant offers.

Long-Term Engagement Automation
CRMs allow dealerships to maintain engagement with leads over extended periods, keeping them warm until they're ready to take the next step.
- **Cold Lead Engagement**: Automate occasional touchpoints for leads who haven't shown immediate interest, keeping the dealership in their mind for future needs.
- **High-Interest Lead Focus**: Increase frequency and personalization for leads showing strong interest, reinforcing their commitment to visiting the dealership.

2.3. SalesLeader: The Only Dealer Sales Management System

While CRMs provide invaluable support in managing digital and remote interactions, **SalesLeader** is the only Dealer Sales Management system designed to take over once the customer arrives at the dealership. Unlike a CRM, SalesLeader manages deals rather than leads and optimizes in-dealership sales activities. This unique role complements the CRM by focusing on maximizing appointment show-ups, conversion rates, and in-store customer engagement.

Real-Time In-Dealership Visibility
SalesLeader provides real-time insights and structure to the in-store sales process, which are vital for managers and sales reps looking to convert showroom visits into sales.

- **Activity Tracking and Efficiency**: Tracks key steps in the in-dealership process, from initial greeting to final close, allowing managers to adjust efforts in real time to keep deals on track.

Structured Sales Cadence for In-Store Processes
SalesLeader guides the sales team through a structured in-store process, keeping customer interactions efficient, engaging, and focused on closing the sale.
- **Step-by-Step Sales Process**: Guides sales reps through each stage of the customer interaction, ensuring that no steps are missed and that the experience is seamless.
- **Closing Optimization**: By organizing necessary steps and documents in a clear order, SalesLeader shortens the sales cycle, allowing reps to close deals more efficiently.

In-Store Performance Tracking
SalesLeader tracks critical in-store performance metrics, such as conversion rates, time to close, and customer satisfaction indicators, helping dealerships identify areas for continuous improvement.
- **Conversion Rate Tracking**: Tracks how often appointments result in a closed sale, giving insight into the effectiveness of in-store processes.
- **Team Performance Metrics**: Allows managers to monitor individual and team performance in real time, identifying training needs and recognizing top performers.

2.4. Maximizing CRM and SalesLeader Synergy for Holistic Engagement

While there is no integration between CRMs and SalesLeader, using these systems together offers a comprehensive approach to managing both digital and in-store interactions, helping dealerships to capture leads, engage customers, and close sales.

Unified Customer Profiles and Handoff Efficiency
By using both CRM and SalesLeader, sales reps gain a full view of each customer's history, from initial inquiry to in-store experience.
- **Seamless Transition from CRM to SalesLeader**: Sales reps can build on CRM-captured data to tailor in-store interactions, ensuring customers feel personally attended to and engaged.
- **Complete Customer Journey Tracking**: From the first point of contact through to the final handshake, dealerships benefit from a cohesive view of each customer's journey.

Streamlined In-Store Sales Cycle with SalesLeader
SalesLeader's focus on managing in-store interactions creates a smooth experience for both the customer and sales team, ensuring customers receive the same high level of service in the showroom as they did in initial digital interactions.
- **Time Efficiency**: SalesLeader organizes the steps in the sales process to keep the timeline tight and reduce waiting times.

Chapter X

- **Focused In-Store Engagement**: Helps the sales team maintain focus and professionalism during high-stakes in-person interactions, leading to higher conversion rates.

2.5. Enhanced Post-Appointment Follow-Ups and Engagement

With the CRM handling follow-ups and SalesLeader supporting a structured in-store experience, dealerships have a solid foundation for re-engaging customers and solidifying relationships post-appointment.

Automated Post-Visit Communication
Following an appointment, CRM systems can send thank-you messages, request feedback, and offer additional information, building on the positive in-store experience facilitated by SalesLeader.
- **Feedback Collection**: Automated surveys capture insights on customer satisfaction, helping dealerships refine their approach.
- **Follow-Up Offers**: Re-engage customers with offers on similar vehicles or accessories based on their expressed interests.

Recovering No-Shows
When a customer misses an appointment, CRMs allow for automated follow-ups, and insights from SalesLeader can guide personalized communication.
- **Encouraging Reschedules**: Friendly follow-up messages prompt no-shows to reschedule, with the CRM handling messaging cadence.
- **Data-Driven Personalization**: Insights from SalesLeader interactions guide tailored messaging, addressing specific objections or preferences.

Conclusion: Combining CRM and SalesLeader for Appointment and Sales Success

By using dealership CRMs and SalesLeader together, dealerships can create a powerful system that combines seamless lead follow-up, structured in-store engagement, and continuous tracking of customer interactions. CRM systems efficiently manage follow-ups, ensuring leads are nurtured and appointments are scheduled, while SalesLeader transforms in-dealership sales by optimizing each step of the in-store process. Together, these complementary tools provide a holistic approach that enhances lead conversion, customer satisfaction, and dealership performance.

Section 3. Optimizing Software for Automated Reminders and Confirmations

In the automotive industry, automated reminders and confirmations are essential tools for ensuring that appointments stay top-of-mind for customers and reducing the likelihood of no-shows. Leveraging the capabilities of dealership-specific CRM systems, dealerships can set up automated workflows that efficiently handle reminders and confirmations, providing a consistent experience for customers. While CRMs play a primary role in these automated communications, SalesLeader enhances

Chapter X

this process by providing in-store management that supports high engagement once the customer arrives.

3.1. Setting Up Automated Reminder and Confirmation Sequences in CRM Systems

Automated reminders and confirmations play a pivotal role in ensuring that customers remember their appointments and arrive prepared. Dealership CRMs, such as VinSolutions, ELEAD1ONE, and DealerSocket, have built-in tools for scheduling these communications in customizable sequences based on the appointment timeline.

Creating Effective Reminders

Well-crafted reminders help reinforce the importance of the appointment and reduce the likelihood of last-minute cancellations or no-shows. CRMs allow dealerships to customize these reminders in terms of timing, content, and delivery method.

- **Pre-Appointment Confirmations**: Send an initial confirmation immediately after scheduling to reinforce the customer's commitment.
- **24-Hour and Same-Day Reminders**: Best practice suggests sending a reminder 24 hours before the appointment and, if appropriate, another one the morning of the appointment. This cadence keeps the appointment top-of-mind without overwhelming the customer.
- **Personalized Messaging**: Tailor reminders to include specific information, such as the vehicle's make and model, the sales representative's name, and dealership location details, which gives customers a clear sense of readiness and professionalism.

Multi-Channel Communication Options

CRMs offer a range of communication options, including email, SMS, and automated voice calls, allowing dealerships to reach customers through their preferred channel.

- **Text Message Reminders**: SMS reminders are especially effective because of their high open rate, making them ideal for both initial confirmations and last-minute reminders.
- **Email Confirmations**: Include appointment details, dealership information, and any additional notes or requirements (such as required documents) to ensure the customer arrives prepared.
- **Automated Voice Calls**: For customers who prefer phone calls, automated voice reminders can provide a more personalized touch, often leaving a strong impression.

3.2. Benefits of CRM-Driven Automated Reminder Cadences

Establishing consistent reminder cadences through CRM automation creates a professional and reliable experience for customers while freeing up dealership staff to focus on higher-level tasks. These reminders also help reduce appointment no-shows, improve operational efficiency, and support a predictable sales pipeline.

Reduction of No-Shows
By keeping customers reminded of their upcoming appointments, CRMs help minimize the occurrence of no-shows, which can otherwise disrupt the dealership's schedule and affect sales performance.
- **Behavioral Cues**: Reminders reinforce the importance of the appointment, subtly reminding customers of the time-sensitive nature of the vehicle they're interested in.
- **Consistency in Communication**: Automated reminders ensure that every customer receives the same level of attention, even during busy periods, which boosts trust in the dealership's professionalism.

Operational Efficiency
With CRMs managing reminders, dealership staff are freed from manually tracking and confirming appointments, enabling them to prioritize direct customer interactions and higher-impact activities.
- **Streamlined Schedules**: Automated reminders help staff anticipate customer arrivals more accurately, creating a smoother flow of appointments.
- **Improved Resource Allocation**: With a reliable reminder cadence, the sales and BDC teams can allocate time and resources more effectively, knowing that customers are likely to show up as planned.

Enhanced Customer Experience
Reminders sent at strategic intervals demonstrate a dealership's commitment to customer satisfaction and follow-through, setting the tone for a positive experience from the very beginning.
- **Clear Instructions and Directions**: CRM systems can automatically include directions, preparation tips, and contact information in reminders, helping customers feel more comfortable and confident about their visit.
- **Responsive Rescheduling Options**: Should the customer need to reschedule, CRM reminders can include rescheduling links or contact information, allowing for a seamless change of plans.

3.3. How SalesLeader Complements CRM Automation for In-Dealership Appointments

While CRM systems manage digital and remote communications, **SalesLeader** focuses on optimizing in-dealership experiences by ensuring that the in-person sales process runs smoothly once a customer arrives. As the only Dealer Sales Management system available, SalesLeader bridges the gap by enhancing engagement and conversion within the dealership, working alongside the CRM to ensure that every appointment is maximized.

In-Store Appointment Management
SalesLeader provides real-time visibility into scheduled appointments and customer arrivals, allowing the sales team to be fully prepared as each appointment time approaches.

- **Arrival Notifications**: Alerts the sales team when a customer arrives, ensuring a prompt greeting and smooth transition into the in-dealership process.
- **Appointment Tracking**: Tracks each customer's progress through the dealership's sales stages, allowing sales reps and managers to monitor engagement and ensure all steps are completed efficiently.

Enhanced Conversion Opportunities

SalesLeader structures the in-store sales process in a way that increases the likelihood of a sale, helping dealerships make the most of every scheduled appointment.

- **Optimized Sales Flow**: Guides the sales team through a step-by-step process, keeping each interaction professional and efficient, which improves the customer's overall experience and increases the probability of closing.
- **Engagement Insights**: Tracks time spent in each part of the sales process, allowing managers to identify potential bottlenecks and make adjustments to maintain momentum.

Feedback for Continuous Improvement

SalesLeader's in-dealership metrics provide insights that help the sales team refine their approach over time, aligning with the CRM's automated outreach to create a seamless customer journey from start to finish.

- **Show Rate Tracking**: Analyzes which types of appointments are more likely to show up and convert, providing data that can refine CRM reminder and follow-up strategies.
- **Performance Benchmarks**: Enables the dealership to assess the effectiveness of in-person interactions, allowing for tailored training and improvement.

3.4. Best Practices for Optimizing Automated Reminders and Confirmations

To make the most of CRM-driven automation, dealerships should consider a few best practices for designing effective reminder and confirmation workflows that align with customer preferences and support SalesLeader's in-store efficiency.

Timing and Frequency

Structure reminders based on when the appointment is scheduled, using well-timed touchpoints to keep the customer engaged without overwhelming them.

- **Initial Confirmation Immediately After Scheduling**: Reinforces commitment right after booking.
- **Reminder 24 Hours in Advance**: Acts as a courtesy reminder for planning.
- **Same-Day Reminder**: For morning appointments, consider an evening reminder the night before; for afternoon appointments, a morning reminder is ideal.

Clear and Concise Messaging

Keep messages short, relevant, and action oriented. Include all necessary details without adding too much information, which may dilute the message.

Chapter X

- **Personalization**: Address the customer by name and mention the vehicle model to make the reminder feel tailored.
- **Action Prompts**: Use language that gently encourages the customer to confirm or reach out if they need to reschedule.

Providing Rescheduling Options
Include a link or contact information for rescheduling, showing flexibility and making it easy for customers to update their plans.

- **Easy Rescheduling Links**: If the CRM supports it, embed a rescheduling link in the reminder for customer convenience.
- **Personal Contact**: For customers who prefer speaking with a team member, add a phone number for rescheduling.

Testing and Adjusting
Continuously assess the effectiveness of reminder cadences, timing, and messaging by analyzing show rates and customer feedback.

- **A/B Testing**: Test different reminder timings or message formats to identify which combinations lead to higher show rates.
- **Data-Driven Adjustments**: Use CRM analytics to identify peak appointment days and times, adjusting reminder timing accordingly.

Conclusion: Maximizing Show Rates with Automated Reminders and SalesLeader's In-Store Optimization

Optimizing automated reminders and confirmations within a dealership's CRM provides customers with a seamless, professional experience before they arrive. By incorporating multi-channel reminders at strategic intervals, dealerships can reinforce appointment commitments and reduce no-show rates. Once the customer arrives, SalesLeader's unique role as the Dealer Sales Management system ensures that in-dealership interactions remain structured and efficient, creating a smooth transition from digital follow-up to in-person engagement. Together, CRM automation and SalesLeader in-store optimization provide a powerful approach that enhances customer satisfaction, maximizes conversions, and reinforces dealership professionalism at every touchpoint.

Chapter XI

BDC Considerations

(Business Development Center)

Section 1. Evaluating Whether a BDC Makes Sense for the Dealership

Establishing a Business Development Center (BDC) can be a significant investment for a dealership, impacting sales, customer service, and operational efficiency. A BDC serves as a dedicated team to handle incoming and outgoing communications, manage leads, and set appointments, freeing up sales staff to focus on in-person interactions. While the benefits of a BDC can be substantial, it's essential for each dealership to carefully assess its specific needs, goals, and resources before committing to a BDC model.

This section explores key factors dealerships should consider when determining if a BDC is the right fit, helping leadership make an informed decision that aligns with the dealership's growth and customer engagement strategies.

1.1. Understanding the Role and Purpose of a BDC

A BDC is a centralized team within a dealership dedicated to managing customer communication, including lead follow-up, appointment setting, and customer service inquiries. The BDC's primary focus is on building relationships with potential and existing customers, nurturing leads, and converting interest into dealership visits.

A well-run BDC can:
- **Increase Appointment Volume**: By proactively contacting leads and following up on inquiries, a BDC can boost the number of appointments set for the sales team.
- **Improve Lead Conversion Rates**: Specialized BDC representatives are trained to handle objections, create urgency, and persuade potential customers to visit the dealership.
- **Enhance Customer Experience**: By offering prompt and personalized communication, a BDC can improve the overall customer experience, making customers feel valued and supported throughout their journey.

Chapter XI

- **Free Up Sales Staff for In-Person Interactions**: Sales staff can focus on closing deals rather than spending time on the phone or responding to online inquiries.

1.2. Key Considerations for Implementing a BDC

Implementing a BDC requires careful planning, as it involves costs, training, and ongoing management. Here are some critical factors to evaluate:

Lead Volume and Market Demand
A BDC makes the most sense for dealerships with high lead volumes. Dealerships in competitive markets or those with substantial digital advertising and lead-generation efforts may benefit significantly from a BDC, as the volume of inquiries can overwhelm sales teams and lead to missed opportunities.

- Assessing Lead Volume: Consider the average monthly inquiries the dealership receives via phone, website, and third-party listing sites. If sales staff struggles to follow up promptly or if lead response times are lagging, a BDC can help manage the workload.
- Market Competitiveness: In markets with intense competition, a BDC can differentiate the dealership by ensuring fast, attentive responses to leads, potentially giving an edge over competitors.

Available Resources and Budget
Setting up a BDC involves costs for staffing, training, technology, and workspace. Dealerships need to assess whether they have the budget to support these expenses and if the potential benefits justify the investment.

- **Cost of Staffing and Training**: A BDC requires trained representatives who can effectively communicate with customers and represent the dealership. Hiring, onboarding, and training these reps, as well as paying competitive salaries, is an investment.
- **Technology and Software Needs**: BDCs often use specialized CRM and communication tools to track leads, monitor calls, and automate follow-ups. Assess whether the dealership's current technology can support a BDC or if new investments will be needed.
- **Physical Space and Equipment**: If operating on-site, the BDC will need a dedicated workspace and equipment. Evaluate if the dealership has the space for a BDC or if remote work is a feasible option.

Sales Staff Bandwidth and Focus
BDC teams alleviate some of the pressure on sales staff by taking on communication and appointment-setting tasks, allowing sales reps to focus more on in-person interactions and closing sales.

- **Current Workload of Sales Staff**: If sales staff are consistently juggling phone calls, emails, and in-person sales tasks, a BDC can relieve them of

initial lead management and follow-up, which can improve focus and efficiency.
- **Impact on Closing Rates**: Allowing sales staff to concentrate on face-to-face interactions may improve their closing rates, as they can devote more attention to each customer without the distraction of handling inbound calls or online inquiries.

Customer Service and Experience Goals

A BDC can enhance the customer experience by ensuring prompt, consistent, and professional communication with potential and existing customers. If customer service is a priority for the dealership, a BDC may help meet these objectives by handling queries quickly and building stronger relationships with leads.

- **Improving Customer Satisfaction**: A dedicated BDC team can provide follow-ups, answer questions, and resolve issues promptly, leading to better customer satisfaction scores.
- **Strengthening Relationships with Repeat Customers**: For dealerships that rely on repeat business, a BDC can manage ongoing communication with existing customers, nurturing long-term relationships and encouraging repeat purchases.

1.3. Evaluating ROI and Performance Metrics

Determining the return on investment (ROI) for a BDC is crucial. Dealerships should establish key performance indicators (KPIs) to assess the effectiveness of the BDC over time. Metrics such as appointment show-up rates, lead response times, and sales conversion rates provide insight into the BDC's impact on the dealership's bottom line.

- **Appointment Show-Up Rates**: Track the percentage of scheduled appointments that result in actual dealership visits. An effective BDC should help improve this rate by building strong rapport with leads.
- **Lead Response Time**: A shorter lead response time can improve conversion rates, as prompt follow-ups indicate attentiveness and increase the likelihood of customer engagement.
- **Sales Conversion Rates**: Compare conversion rates for customers who interacted with the BDC versus those who didn't. This comparison can help determine if the BDC is improving lead quality and facilitating successful sales.

1.4. Weighing the Pros and Cons of a BDC for Your Dealership

Before deciding to implement a BDC, it's essential to weigh the potential benefits against the associated costs and operational changes. Here are some key pros and cons to consider:

Pros of a BDC:

Chapter XI

- **Increased Efficiency**: The BDC can handle lead nurturing, appointment setting, and follow-ups, freeing sales staff to focus on closing.
- **Enhanced Customer Experience**: With a dedicated team for inbound and outbound communications, customer service levels may improve, leading to better customer retention and satisfaction.
- **Better Lead Conversion**: A well-trained BDC team can build relationships with leads, increasing the likelihood that they'll visit the dealership and complete a purchase.

Cons of a BDC:
- **Upfront and Ongoing Costs**: Staffing, training, technology, and workspace costs add up and can strain budgets if lead volume doesn't justify the expense.
- **Management and Oversight Requirements**: A BDC requires consistent oversight to ensure that representatives are following protocols, providing quality service, and meeting performance goals.
- **Potential for Disconnect**: If not managed well, the handoff from the BDC to the sales team can lead to communication gaps, especially if the customer has to repeat information or if the sales team doesn't receive a clear summary of the lead.

Conclusion: Is a BDC Right for Your Dealership?

Deciding whether to implement a BDC is a strategic choice that depends on a dealership's lead volume, budget, and customer engagement goals. Dealerships with high lead volumes, significant market competition, and a strong commitment to customer service may find that a BDC offers measurable benefits. However, smaller dealerships or those with limited budgets might find that a streamlined in-house approach to handling leads is more effective.

A clear understanding of the BDC's potential impact, combined with a well-thought-out plan for implementation, can help dealerships determine if this model aligns with their goals. Evaluating the dealership's unique needs and resources ensures that the decision is made with confidence and that any BDC implemented is well-positioned to drive growth, enhance customer experience, and improve efficiency.

Section 2. Setting Up and Managing a BDC for Success

Once a dealership decides to implement a Business Development Center (BDC), careful planning and management are essential for maximizing its effectiveness. A well-structured BDC can drive more appointments, enhance lead conversion, and improve customer satisfaction. However, setting up a BDC involves more than simply hiring staff; it requires defining roles, training representatives, implementing the right technology, and establishing clear performance metrics. This section provides a roadmap for setting up and managing a successful BDC, covering team structure, processes, technology, and performance tracking.

2.1. Building the BDC Team

A BDC's success depends heavily on the people running it. From managers to representatives, every team member plays a vital role in ensuring smooth operations, effective communication with leads, and a high level of customer service.

Hiring the Right Team Members
BDC representatives need excellent communication skills, empathy, resilience, and a customer-focused mindset. They are often the first point of contact for leads, so their interactions shape first impressions and can strongly influence a customer's decision to visit the dealership.

- **Ideal BDC Representative Traits**: Strong verbal communication, listening skills, patience, ability to handle objections, adaptability, and a persuasive yet professional tone.
- **BDC Manager Qualifications**: The BDC manager should have experience in lead management, sales, and customer service. They will be responsible for overseeing daily operations, coaching representatives, and ensuring that processes are followed consistently.

Defining Roles and Responsibilities
Clear role definitions help prevent overlap, reduce confusion, and establish accountability within the BDC team.

- **BDC Representatives**: Responsible for answering inbound calls, handling online inquiries, setting appointments, and following up with leads. Their goal is to build rapport, create urgency, and encourage showroom visits.
- **BDC Manager**: Oversees the team, monitors performance metrics, provides coaching and feedback, and ensures that representatives are trained to handle inquiries effectively. The manager also coordinates with sales staff to ensure a smooth handoff of leads.

Setting Up an Effective Onboarding and Training Program
BDC representatives require comprehensive training that covers both product knowledge and communication techniques. A strong onboarding program can increase confidence, improve job satisfaction, and reduce turnover.

- **Product and Service Training**: Ensure that representatives understand the dealership's inventory, current promotions, financing options, and any unique dealership selling points.
- **Communication Skills Training**: Equip representatives with skills in active listening, empathy, objection handling, and urgency creation. Role-playing exercises can help them practice common scenarios and develop effective responses.
- **Technology and CRM Training**: Representatives should be comfortable using the dealership's CRM system and any other lead management tools to log interactions, track lead status, and schedule appointments efficiently.

Chapter XI

2.2. Implementing Processes for Lead Management and Follow-Up

To maintain consistency and ensure no leads fall through the cracks, the BDC should have a clearly defined process for lead handling and follow-up.

Establishing a Lead Handling Workflow
A standardized workflow helps representatives manage leads effectively, from the initial inquiry through follow-up and appointment setting. The workflow should cover:

- **Lead Categorization**: Segment leads based on source, inquiry type, or level of interest. For instance, a lead from a website form may require different follow-up steps than an inbound phone call.
- **Lead Response Time**: Define acceptable response times for different lead types. Ideally, all inquiries should receive a response within a few minutes, as quicker responses can significantly improve conversion rates.
- **Scripts and Guidelines**: Provide scripts and guidelines for common scenarios, such as availability checks, pricing inquiries, and trade-in requests. Standardized responses ensure that all leads receive accurate information and a consistent experience.

Follow-Up Schedule and Strategy
Following up on leads at regular intervals helps maintain interest and maximizes the chance of scheduling an appointment. Create a structured follow-up schedule that BDC representatives can follow based on lead type and engagement level.

- **Initial Follow-Up**: Follow up on all leads within the first 24 hours if the initial contact didn't result in an appointment.
- **Subsequent Follow-Ups**: Schedule additional follow-ups at set intervals (e.g., 3 days, 1 week, and 2 weeks) depending on the lead's responsiveness and engagement.
- **Customized Follow-Up**: Encourage representatives to personalize follow-ups based on previous interactions, such as mentioning a vehicle or feature the customer expressed interest in. Personalization increases the effectiveness of follow-ups by demonstrating attention to customer preferences.

2.3. Technology and Tools to Support the BDC
The right technology infrastructure is crucial for BDC efficiency and productivity. From tracking leads to scheduling appointments, technology can streamline operations and provide valuable insights into performance.

Customer Relationship Management (CRM) System
A robust CRM is the backbone of a BDC, enabling representatives to log interactions, track lead status, and manage follow-ups. A CRM also helps integrate BDC operations with the sales team, ensuring that leads are seamlessly handed off.

- **CRM Requirements for a BDC**: Look for a CRM that offers lead tracking, automated reminders for follow-ups, detailed customer profiles, and easy integration with other dealership software. Real-time updates are essential to keep information synchronized across the BDC and sales teams.

Communication Tools
Effective communication tools support both inbound and outbound efforts. Call-tracking systems, email templates, and messaging platforms enable representatives to manage inquiries efficiently.

- **Call-Tracking and Analytics**: Call-tracking software records call details, allowing the BDC to monitor response times, call outcomes, and quality. Analytics help assess representative performance and identify areas for improvement.
- **Email and Text Templates**: Pre-written email and text templates for common scenarios save time and ensure consistent communication. Templates can be customized to fit each customer interaction, such as confirming appointments or sending follow-up reminders.

c. Performance Tracking and Reporting Tools
Performance-tracking tools allow managers to monitor metrics, assess effectiveness, and optimize BDC operations. Dashboards and reporting features in the CRM can provide real-time insights into metrics such as appointment-setting rates, lead response times, and conversion rates.

- **Real-Time Dashboards**: Visual dashboards make it easy to track KPIs and identify areas for improvement, such as follow-up effectiveness or lead response times.
- **Regular Reporting**: Weekly or monthly reports help evaluate long-term trends, identify top-performing representatives, and make data-driven decisions for the BDC.

2.4. Performance Metrics to Monitor and Improve BDC Effectiveness

Regularly monitoring performance metrics allows the dealership to measure the BDC's impact and identify areas for improvement. Key performance indicators (KPIs) offer insights into how well the BDC is meeting goals and can help drive decisions around staffing, training, and process adjustments.

Key Metrics to Track:
- **Appointment Setting Rate**: The percentage of leads that result in scheduled appointments. A high appointment-setting rate indicates effective communication and follow-up by the BDC.
- **Appointment Show-Up Rate**: The percentage of scheduled appointments that lead to dealership visits. This metric highlights the quality of the BDC's appointment setting and urgency creation efforts.

- **Lead Response Time**: The average time it takes for representatives to respond to inquiries. Faster response times correlate with higher lead engagement and conversion.
- **Follow-Up Conversion Rate**: The percentage of follow-ups that result in appointments or further engagement. This metric evaluates the effectiveness of the BDC's follow-up strategy.
- **Customer Satisfaction Score**: Feedback from customers on their BDC experience. High satisfaction scores reflect positive interactions and support the dealership's reputation.

2.5. Ensuring Alignment with the Sales Team

A successful BDC requires seamless coordination with the sales team. The BDC's goal is to set high-quality appointments that lead to in-person interactions, so alignment with sales is essential for maximizing conversion rates.

Strategies for BDC-Sales Alignment:
- **Daily or Weekly Briefings**: Regular meetings between the BDC and sales team ensure alignment on leads, appointments, and follow-up strategies. Briefings allow teams to exchange updates and address any challenges.
- **Clear Handoff Process**: Ensure that all information collected by the BDC is shared with the sales team to avoid duplicate questions and provide a smooth customer experience.
- **Feedback Loop**: Encourage sales reps to provide feedback on the quality of leads and appointments set by the BDC. This input can help the BDC refine their approach, improving lead quality and conversion rates.

Conclusion: Setting Up a BDC for Long-Term Success

Implementing a BDC can transform lead management and improve the dealership's bottom line, but it requires thorough planning, training, and alignment with sales. By hiring the right team, defining clear processes, leveraging effective technology, and monitoring performance, dealerships can ensure that their BDC functions efficiently and delivers results. Consistent performance tracking and strong communication between the BDC and sales teams support a seamless, high-quality customer journey from the first inquiry to the showroom visit.

Section 3. Best Practices for Effective Communication Between the BDC and the Sales Team

For a Business Development Center (BDC) to deliver its full value, communication between the BDC and the sales team must be seamless and collaborative. Effective communication ensures that leads are handed off smoothly, representatives are well-informed, and customer experiences are consistent from initial inquiry to final purchase. Misalignment or poor communication between the two teams can result in missed opportunities, misunderstandings, and a disjointed customer experience. This section explores best practices to establish a productive and synchronized relationship between the BDC and sales teams.

3.1. Establishing a Clear Handoff Process

A structured handoff process helps ensure that BDC representatives pass on all necessary information to the sales team, reducing the need for customers to repeat themselves and allowing sales reps to pick up the conversation where the BDC left off.

Key Elements of an Effective Handoff:
- **Standardized Information Sharing**: Define the specific information that BDC representatives should gather and share with sales, such as the customer's preferred vehicle, any stated preferences or concerns, and relevant contact details.
- **Lead Handoff Documentation**: Use CRM notes or handoff templates to document lead interactions in a way that's easily accessible to the sales team. Include key details like the lead's inquiry type, urgency level, and appointment time.
- **Real-Time Updates**: For high-priority leads or last-minute appointments, notify sales immediately to ensure the rep is prepared. Real-time updates help minimize missed opportunities and ensure reps are ready when customers arrive.

Example Handoff Checklist:
- Customer's name and contact information
- Vehicle or service of interest
- Customer's expressed preferences (features, budget, color, etc.)
- Lead source and how they found the dealership (website, referral, etc.)
- Date and time of the scheduled appointment

3.2. Regular Meetings and Briefings

Frequent meetings and briefings allow both teams to stay updated on lead quality, conversion rates, and any new initiatives. These sessions create a collaborative environment where both sides can provide feedback, address challenges, and align on goals.

Types of Meetings:
- **Daily Standups**: Short daily check-ins keep both teams informed of new leads, high-priority appointments, and potential scheduling conflicts.
- **Weekly Performance Reviews**: Weekly meetings can focus on lead conversion rates, challenges faced during the handoff process, and feedback from recent appointments. These reviews provide an opportunity to refine processes and improve overall performance.
- **Monthly Strategy Meetings**: Monthly meetings are ideal for discussing broader strategies, evaluating key metrics, and implementing long-term improvements to the BDC-sales process.

Meeting Agenda Suggestions:
- Review of upcoming high-priority appointments
- Feedback on recent handoffs and customer interactions
- Discussion of any new promotions, inventory changes, or policy updates
- Open feedback and suggestions for improving communication

3.3. Creating a Feedback Loop Between BDC and Sales

A feedback loop ensures that both teams can learn from each other's experiences, leading to continuous improvement. Sales reps can provide insights into the quality of appointments set by the BDC, while the BDC can use this feedback to refine their lead management practices.

Feedback Loop Best Practices:
- **Encourage Open Communication**: Foster a culture where feedback is constructive and welcomed by both teams. Create a system where sales reps can easily share insights about the quality of leads or the effectiveness of BDC communications.
- **Use a Structured Format**: A structured format for feedback, such as a monthly feedback form or regular performance reports, can help both teams identify trends and adjust strategies accordingly.
- **Highlight Success Stories and Areas for Improvement**: Celebrate successful handoffs and customer interactions while addressing any patterns that need improvement. For instance, if certain lead types convert better than others, the BDC can prioritize these in follow-ups.

Example Feedback Questions for Sales to BDC:
- Was the lead adequately prepared with relevant information before the appointment?
- Were any crucial details missing that could have improved the appointment?
- Did the customer seem well-informed and engaged when they arrived?
- Any specific suggestions for improving lead handoffs?

3.4 Aligning Goals and Incentives

When both teams share common goals, they're more likely to collaborate effectively. Establishing shared objectives and aligning incentives fosters a team-oriented culture where everyone is working toward the same outcome: maximizing conversions and creating positive customer experiences.

Suggested Shared Goals:
- **Appointment Show-Up Rate**: The percentage of scheduled appointments that result in dealership visits can serve as a primary performance indicator for both teams.
- **Conversion Rate**: Track the conversion rate for BDC-set appointments to measure the impact of both teams' efforts in closing sales.

- **Customer Satisfaction Scores**: Feedback from customers on their experience with both the BDC and sales teams provides insights into the overall quality of interactions and helps refine processes.

Incentive Ideas for BDC and Sales Alignment:
- **Bonus for High Show-Up Rates**: A bonus structure based on appointment show-up rates encourages the BDC to set qualified appointments and the sales team to keep customers engaged.
- **Shared Conversion Goals**: Set monthly conversion goals and reward both teams if they achieve or exceed the target, promoting teamwork and accountability.
- **Customer Satisfaction Rewards**: High customer satisfaction scores reflect well on both teams and should be recognized with rewards, reinforcing the importance of a smooth, positive customer journey.

3.5 Utilizing CRM for Transparent Communication

A CRM system acts as the central hub for all lead interactions, ensuring that both the BDC and sales teams have access to the same information and can see updates in real-time. Proper CRM usage streamlines communication and minimizes misunderstandings.

CRM Best Practices for BDC-Sales Communication:
- **Detailed Lead Notes**: BDC representatives should log every customer interaction with comprehensive notes, including key points discussed, customer preferences, and next steps. Sales reps should review these notes before appointments to understand the customer's background.
- **Appointment Reminders and Notifications**: Set up CRM notifications for upcoming appointments, last-minute changes, or follow-up reminders to keep both teams on the same page.
- **Automated Handoff Alerts**: Use automated alerts to notify sales reps of new appointments or important updates in real-time, so they're always aware of incoming leads and appointments.

Example CRM Workflow:
- **Step 1**: BDC representative logs the lead's information, inquiry type, and any specific details discussed.
- **Step 2**: An automated alert notifies the assigned sales rep of the new lead and upcoming appointment.
- **Step 3**: Sales rep reviews the lead information and follows up as needed, marking the outcome of the appointment in the CRM.
- **Step 4**: The CRM tracks lead status changes, and performance metrics can be easily accessed for both teams.

3.6 Maintaining a Culture of Collaboration and Respect

Chapter XI

Successful communication between the BDC and sales teams depends on a culture of mutual respect and collaboration. Each team plays a vital role in the customer journey, and it's essential that they appreciate each other's contributions.

Strategies for Building a Collaborative Culture:
- **Encourage Team Bonding**: Organize occasional joint team-building activities to strengthen relationships and foster camaraderie.
- **Celebrate Successes Together**: When key milestones are met (e.g., monthly conversion targets or customer satisfaction goals), celebrate achievements as a team to reinforce shared accomplishments.
- **Address Challenges Respectfully**: If issues arise, address them openly and professionally, focusing on solutions rather than blame. An environment that encourages constructive problem-solving is essential for maintaining a positive, high-performing team dynamic.

Example Team Bonding Activity:
- **Monthly Recognition Awards**: Recognize both BDC and sales team members who contributed to exceptional customer experiences, appointment conversions, or other successes. This mutual acknowledgment fosters a supportive team environment.

Conclusion: Creating a Unified BDC-Sales Experience

Effective communication between the BDC and sales teams is crucial for delivering a smooth and professional customer experience. By establishing clear handoff processes, fostering open feedback, aligning goals, and leveraging CRM tools, dealerships can ensure that both teams work together seamlessly. Building a culture of respect, collaboration, and shared success enables the BDC and sales team to function as a cohesive unit, driving growth, customer satisfaction, and overall dealership success.

Section 4. Compensation Models – Structuring Pay to Incentivize Successful Appointments and Show-Ups

An effective BDC compensation model should account for the variety and volume of leads a representative handles, from inbound calls and internet inquiries to outreach for maturing leases and expiring warranties. These different lead types require varying levels of engagement and follow-up, impacting the rep's overall productivity and success. The following model is designed to motivate BDC reps to handle a balanced volume of leads while prioritizing high-quality interactions that drive appointments, show-ups, and sales conversions.

4.1. BDC Role and Lead Expectations

A BDC representative is typically responsible for managing a blend of inbound calls, internet leads, and proactive follow-ups on customers with maturing leases or expiring service contracts. The number of leads a rep can handle effectively each month depends on the lead type, source, and hours worked. For example, inbound calls from interested buyers generally convert more easily than third-party leads shared with multiple dealerships, so performance expectations and compensation should reflect these differences.

Monthly Lead Handling Expectations:
- **Blended Inbound and Internet Leads**: Approximately 175 new leads per month, including calls, internet leads.
- **Appointment-Setting Rate**: 40% of leads should convert into scheduled appointments.
- **Show-Up Rate**: At least 50% of appointments should result in customer visits.
- **Appointments-to-Sale Rate**: At least 60% of show-ups should convert into sales.

Based on these metrics, a typical BDC rep should aim to set around 70 appointments each month, resulting in 35 show-ups, with approximately 21 cars sold to achieve minimum performance standards.

4.2. Recommended Compensation Plan: Base as Draw Against Compensation

Compensation Structure:
- **Base Pay (Draw)**: $15 per hour, totaling approximately $2,600 monthly for full-time (40-hour/week) reps. This is a guaranteed base that acts as a draw against earned compensation and bonuses.
- **Appointment Show-Up Compensation**: $50 for each appointment that results in a customer visit.
- **Sales Conversion Bonus**: $50 for each appointment that converts into a sale.

Example Monthly Earnings Calculation:

Expected Earnings Ranges:

Scenario 1: *29 Shows and 16 Sales*

Calculations:
Draw: $15/hour x 40 hours/week x 4.33 weeks = $2,600
Show-Up Compensation: 29 show-ups x $50 = $1,450
Sales Conversion Comp: 16 Sales x $50 = $800.
Total Monthly Earnings: $2,250, does not exceed the $2,600 draw received

Scenario 2: *35 Shows and 21 Sales*

Calculations:
Draw: $15/hour x 40 hours/week x 4.33 weeks = $2,600
Show-Up Compensation: 29 show-ups x $50 = $1,750
Sales Conversion Compensation: 16 Sales x $50 = $1050.
Total Monthly Earnings: $2,850, exceeds the $2,600 draw received

Chapter XI

Scenario 3: *40 Shows and 30 Sales*

Calculations:
    Draw: $15/hour x 40 hours/week x 4.33 weeks = $2,600
    Show-Up Compensation: 40 show-ups x $50 = $2,000
    Sales Conversion Compensation: 30 Sales x $50 = $1,500
Total Monthly Earnings: $3,500, exceeds the $2,600 draw received

4.3. Alternative Compensation Plan: Base Pay (no draw) plus Compensation

Compensation Structure:
- **Base Pay**: $10 per hour (not a draw)
- **Appointment Show-Up Bonus**:
  0–35 Show-Ups: $20 per show-up
  35+ Show-Ups: $50 per show-up (retro to 1)
- **Sales Conversion Bonus**: Additional $50 per sale (retro to 1) if the monthly target of 20 sales is achieved.

Let's calculate the monthly earnings for the BDC representative under two different scenarios with this same compensation structure:

Scenario 1: *29 Shows and 16 Sales*
In this scenario, the BDC rep does not meet the sales target of 20 cars sold, so they will not receive the Sales Conversion Bonus.

Calculations
    Base Pay: $10/hour x 40 hours/week x 4.33 weeks = $1,732
    Show-Up Bonus: 29 show-ups x $20 (since they fall into the 0-35 range) = $580
    Sales Conversion Bonus: No bonus, as the 20-sale threshold is not met.
Total Monthly Earnings = $1,732 (base) + $580 (show-up bonus) = **$2,312**

Scenario 2: *40 Shows and 30 Sales*
In this scenario, the BDC rep exceeds the sales target of 20 cars sold, so they qualify for the Sales Conversion Bonus. Additionally, since they have 40 shows, they fall into the higher tier for the Show-Up Bonus.

Calculations
    Base Pay: $10/hour x 40 hours/week x 4.33 weeks = $1,732
    Show-Up Bonus: 40 show-ups x $50 = $2,000
    Sales Conversion Bonus: 25 sales x $50 = $1,250
Total Monthly Earnings = $1,600 (base) + $1,200 (show-up bonus) + $1,500 (sales bonus) = **$4,982**

4.4. Setting Clear Performance Targets and Expectations

To ensure BDC reps understand their goals and incentives, dealerships should set and communicate clear performance metrics based on historical data and dealership-specific needs.

Key Targets to Monitor:
- **Lead Volume**: Based on expected monthly lead types and volumes (e.g., inbound calls, internet inquiries, follow-ups on service and warranty expirations).
- **Appointment Rate**: Targeted appointment-setting rate of 40%.
- **Show-Up Rate**: Minimum of 50% show rate for scheduled appointments.
- **Sales Conversion**: Expected conversion rate of 60% for appointments that show up.

5. Best Practices for Implementing and Maintaining Compensation Models

- **Regular Monitoring and Adjustments**
  Consistently track performance metrics such as show-up and conversion rates to ensure that the compensation structure aligns with dealership goals. Adjust bonuses as needed to stay competitive and motivating.

- **Clear Communication on Compensation Structure**
  Ensure that all BDC representatives understand how their pay is calculated, including how the draw works and how bonuses are earned based on appointment show-ups and sales conversions.

- **Provide Regular Feedback and Support**
  Hold monthly or quarterly check-ins to review reps' performance, provide coaching, and offer constructive feedback on appointment-setting techniques. This feedback loop helps reps stay engaged and improves performance.

- **Recognize and Reward Top Performers**
  Recognize high-performing BDC reps who consistently exceed targets with additional awards, such as "BDC Rep of the Month," to foster a competitive but supportive environment that rewards excellence.

Conclusion: Structuring Pay to Encourage Quality Appointments and Conversions

The recommended compensation model, offering $15 per hour as a draw against a $50 show-up compensation, is designed to encourage BDC reps to prioritize quality appointments that convert into showroom visits and sales. This structure aligns with dealership goals by rewarding the key milestones that drive revenue, while still providing a secure base pay. By setting clear expectations, offering performance-driven bonuses, and providing regular feedback, dealerships can maintain a motivated, high-performing BDC team that contributes to sustained growth and customer satisfaction.

Chapter XI

Chapter XI

Dealers and Associations may contact Chris Cunningham for training or speaking, or to learn more about the SalesLeader DSM (Dealers Sales Management system).

By Phone: (910) 528-1421

By Email: chris@dealersalesleader.com

Website: www.dealersalesleader.com

LinkedIn: https://www.linkedin.com/in/christopherjcunningham

www.ingramcontent.com/pod-product-compliance
Lightning Source LLC
Chambersburg PA
CBHW071516220526
45472CB00003B/1046